Y0-BOH-444

The
Garland Library
of
War and Peace

The
Garland Library
of
War and Peace

Under the General Editorship of

Blanche Wiesen Cook, *John Jay College, C.U.N.Y.*

Sandi E. Cooper, *Richmond College, C.U.N.Y.*

Charles Chatfield, *Wittenberg University*

343.73
C 815c

Conscience and the State

Legal and Administrative Problems
of Conscientious Objectors, 1943-1944

printed with

The Conscientious Objector and the Law

by

Julien Cornell

with a new introduction
for the Garland Edition by
John O'Sullivan

Garland Publishing, Inc., New York & London

1973

WITHDRAWN
HIEBERT LIBRARY
PACIFIC COLLEGE - M. B. SEMINARY
FRESNO. CALIF. 93702
35858

The new introduction for this

Garland Library Edition is Copyright © 1973, by

Garland Publishing Inc.

———

All Rights Reserved

———

Library of Congress Cataloging in Publication Data

Cornell, Julien D   1910-
    Conscience and the state.

    (Garland library of war and peace)
    1. Conscientious objectors--Law and legislation--
United States.   I.   Cornell, Julien D., 1910-
The conscientious objector and the law.   1973.
II. Title.   III.   Title: The conscientious objector
and the law.   IV.   Series.
KF7266.C6C6 1973   343'.73'012   70-147636
ISBN 0-8240-0412-4

Printed in the United States of America

Introduction

Julien Cornell's The Conscientious Objector and the Law *and* Conscience and the State *are essentially campaign polemics and, as such, contain all of the virtues and some of the shortcomings of that genre. The first volume,* The Conscientious Objector and the Law, *examines the provisions of the 1940 Selective Training and Service Act which affected conscientious objectors and the application of that law up until 1943; the subsequent volume,* Conscience and the State, *carries that exploration up through 1944. The multiple themes are often cogently presented and persuasively argued; however, the narrowness of the time frame, 1940-1944, and the episodic tone leave the contemporary reader with a fragmentary awareness of the status of conscientious objectors as America intensified its war effort. The particular strength of the volumes, however, lies in the perceptive analysis of the labyrinthine pathways of selective service administrative procedure. Cornell's delineation of the arbitrary and procedurally inadequate application of the legal provisions governing conscientious objectors makes these volumes necessary reading for anyone who wishes a full understanding of the nation's treatment of conscientious objectors during World War II.*

5

INTRODUCTION

Cornell, a New York attorney, had actively opposed the enactment of peacetime conscription in 1940. Once it became law, he became counsel to the National Committee on Conscientious Objectors of the American Civil Liberties Union and initiated a series of legal challenges to the narrow compass of the conscientious objector provision.

The status of conscientious objectors under the 1940 act, although less than fully satisfactory, marked a clear advance over their abysmal treatment during World War I. The earlier law had limited that classification to members of the historic peace churches; the 1940 enactment expanded the classification to include all who were opposed to participating in war because of religious training and belief. The second major alteration in the status of conscientious objectors concerned the types of permissible service. Under the 1917 act, the only option available was service in a noncombatant capacity; under the 1940 law, provision was made for alternative service in work of national importance under civilian direction.

The 1940 act then, viewed in the context of the traditional American treatment of those who conscientiously refused to take up arms, seems a humane and enlightened document. It still, however, fell considerably short of the British policy, embodied in the National Service Act of 1939, which allowed the absolutist objector, whose conscience would not yield to the dictates of a war-making state, to be exempted from service.

INTRODUCTION

The improved treatment of conscientious objectors under the 1940 act is attributable, in large measure, to the active involvement of church, peace, and civil liberties groups in formulating the law and influencing its administration. The Burke-Wadsworth bill, introduced in June, 1940, virtually repeated the harsh World War I requirements for conscientious objector status. A concerted effort by these groups, both in testifying before the military affairs committees and in extensive lobbying, resulted in a law which was much more responsive to the needs of conscientious objectors.

This campaign of persuasion continued as the Selective Service System undertook to organize the Civilian Public Service camps for those committed to alternative non-military service. The Quakers, Mennonites, Brethren, and Methodists engaged in extensive discussion and negotiation with the government over the administration of the camps.[1] This collaboration, with its hint of co-optation, seemed to some an inappropriate role for the churches. A Mennonite historian, Melvin Gingerich, in describing his church's activity in this area, alluded to the charges that a "nonresistant people" should never petition the government, and that Christ and His Apostles never sought favorable laws from the government. Gingerich, however, agreed with most other observers that this "positive approach" on the part of the churches proved, on balance, beneficial.[2] Of the 151 Civilian Public Service camps ultimately set up under the law, all but four were administered by the peace churches acting as private agencies under the aegis of the Selective Service System.

Although only half as many conscientious objectors, approximately 12,000, served in the Civilian Public Service camps as entered the military in a noncombatant capacity, it is to these men and their situation that Cornell devotes the greatest attention.

The provision for alternative service under civilian direction seemed, to most uncritical observers, to prove the government's good faith. Professor John Masland of Stanford University, writing in August, 1942, regarded the placing of the "responsibility for the discharge of the public duty of those conscientiously opposed to noncombatant service . . . in the hands of his own kind" as "convincing evidence of sympathetic treatment."³ Julian Cornell and many of the participants in the Civilian Public Service camps program challenged Masland's assumption.

There was, to begin with, the issue of military control of the camps. Although individually administered by civilians, the camps were under the jurisdiction of the Selective Service System, headed by General Lewis B. Hershey, and more immediately under the control of the Camp Operations Division, which was run by Colonel Lewis Kosch. Cornell attacked this arrangement as being "most objectionable to pacifists," but the courts proved unresponsive to this claim. In the Roodenko case, which was decided after the publication of Cornell's volumes, the Tenth Circuit Court of Appeals ruled that an activity can be directed by a military man and still be defined as civilian. The ultimate test was whether the participants in the program were subject to military law and, since in the Civilian Public Service program they were not, military direction was allowed to continue.[4]

Although this decision proved bothersome to many working in alternative service, a far greater hardship was the denial of pay to them for their labor and the refusal of the government to provide dependency allotments for their families. Cornell treats, at some length, the injustice of this situation, and the unwillingness of the Selective Service System to resolve this dilemma. This policy of the Selective Service System reflected a very conscious decision to treat the conscientious objectors with benign neglect. General Hershey, assuming that there was widespread public antagonism toward the Civilian Public Service program, decided to give it a very low profile. Testifying before the Senate Military Affairs Committee in 1943, Hershey recounted some of the extraordinary accomplishments of the men in the Civilian Public Service program, but went on to warn that "they must not be allowed to get too much credit for it. It isn't too good for them. I wouldn't want the press to report this."[5] *The lack of pay and allowances, then, regardless of what it meant for the conscientious objectors and their families, served as a valuable public relations device.*

General Hershey's assumption of widespread disaffection for conscientious objectors seems to have been misguided. A public opinion study conducted by Professor Leo Crespi of Princeton University revealed that "the largest proportion of the public expresses no rejection of the conscientious objectors whatsoever, and more than a majority would accept them during this war as closely as friends or closer."[6] If the Selective Service System had not prejudged public opinion and established the Civilian Public Service program in such a way as to deflect the expected criticism about coddling slackers, many of the weaknesses of the program would not have developed. Had, according to one commentator, "the general public been consulted and obeyed, COs would have been paid, received dependency allotments, been allowed to apply their skills, talents and education, and those who wished would have been permitted overseas service in relief and reconstruction."[7]

The Civilian Public Service program existed as an improved, but still essentially flawed, instrument for dealing with conscientious objectors. Julien Cornell, writing in 1944, referred to "defects in the arrangement" that "have become increasingly grave." As the war progressed, these inadequacies in the program evoked increased antagonism from the participants. The Selective Service System, in its official account of the Civilian Public Service camps, acknowledged the "difficulties of extremely critical nature" created by growing resistance in the camps, which "tended to cast disrepute upon the whole first effort of the United States in work of national importance under civilian direction."[8]

Cornell's The Conscientious Objector and the Law *and* Conscience and the State *pinpoint the sources for the discontent within the Civilian Public Service program. Written* in medias res, *these volumes are a probing and often passionate indictment of the shortcomings of the alternative service system. They fail to provide the comprehensive portrait offered by Mulford Sibley and Philip Jacob in* Conscription of Conscience,[9] *but present instead a powerful and moving sense of immediacy. Their ultimate* raison d'etre, *however, is as a needed corrective to the self-congratulatory tone of the Selective Service System's account of the treatment of conscientious objectors during World War II.*

John O'Sullivan
Department of History
Florida Atlantic University

INTRODUCTION

NOTES

[1] *The best account of these negotiations is contained in National Service Board for Religious Objectors,* The Origins of Civilian Public Service *(Washington, D.C., n.d.).*

[2] *Melvin Gingerich, "The Mennonite Church in World War Two: A Review and Evaluation,"* The Mennonite Quarterly Review, *XXV (July, 1951), 186.*

[3] *John W. Masland, Jr., "Treatment of the Conscientious Objector Under the Selective Service Act of 1940,"* American Political Science Review, *XXXVI (August, 1942), 701.*

[4] Roodenko v. United States, *147 F. 2d 752 (1944).*

[5] *78th Congress, First Session, Senate Committee on Military Affairs,* Hearings on S. 763 *(Washington, 1943), 137-138.*

[6] *Leo P. Crespi, "Public Opinion Toward Conscientious Objectors: III, Intensity of Social Rejection in Social Stereotype and Attitude,"* Journal of Psychology, *XIX (April, 1945), 260.*

[7] *Markam P. Bryant, "The Thirteen Thousand,"* The Antioch Review, *VII (March, 1947), 96.*

[8] *Selective Service System,* Conscientious Objection, *Special Monograph No. 11, Volume I (Washington, D.C., 1950), 230.*

[9] *Mulford Q. Sibley and Philip E. Jacob,* Conscription of Conscience: The American State and the Conscientious Objector, *1940-1947 (Ithaca, N.Y., 1952).*

CONSCIENCE AND THE STATE

Legal and Administrative Problems of Conscientious Objectors, 1943-1944

JULIEN CORNELL

Member of the New York Bar, Counsel to the National Committee on Conscientious Objectors of the American Civil Liberties Union.

Published by the Author · *Distributed by*

The John Day Company · New York

By Julien Cornell

The Conscientious Objector and The Law — *1943*
Conscience and The State — *October, 1944*

Distributed by The John Day Company

Copyright, 1944, by Julien Cornell
Manufactured in the United States of America

Contents

Preface

SINCE *The Conscientious Objector and the Law* was published in October, 1943, rapid changes have taken place both in the administration of the law with regard to conscientious objectors and its interpretation by the courts. It is therefore my hope that this volume, a sequel to my earlier work, will prove valuable as well as interesting. While the present work is complete in itself, those who wish to delve more deeply into the background of the subject will want to read also its predecessor.

JULIEN CORNELL.

New York,
September, 1944.

Chapter 1

Civilian Public Service, Now and Hereafter

WHEN THE DRAFT LAW was enacted, Congress did not specify what was to be done with conscientious objectors, but merely provided that those who object even to non-combatant service in the armed forces are to be assigned to "work of national importance under civilian direction."*

The responsibility for deciding to what work conscientious objectors should be assigned rests upon the President, who is given the authority to carry out the draft law by promulgating regulations. This authority he delegated to the Director of Selective Service, who proceeded to set up a system of work camps for conscientious objectors which have become known as "Civilian Public Service" camps.

This being a field in which the government had no experience to draw upon, although compulsory labor camps were common enough in Europe, it was decided to allow the camps to be operated by private agencies: the service organizations of the three pacifist churches, the Brethren, Mennonites and the Society of Friends (Quakers), while the work projects would be supervised by technical agencies of the government such as the Forest Service and the Department of Agriculture, the

---

* Sec. 5(g) Selective Training and Service Act of 1940.

1

whole being under the control of the Director of Selective Service.

There were some dissenters among the pacifist groups, particularly among the Quakers, who felt that it was wrong for them to help administer conscription. British Quakers had refused to do so on the ground that the administration of compulsory work projects would be contrary to their belief in individual freedom, as well as violating their historic position in regard to war. However, these doubts were resolved in favor of the scheme in order to keep the men under control of sympathetic leaders and to avoid the possibility of army-operated camps. The educational possibilities of the plan also influenced its adoption. Thus was born the now familiar Civilian Public Service system.

During the past year, certain defects in the arrangement have become increasingly grave. Foremost of these is the fact that the men are not allowed to obtain jobs for which they are suited—as in England where they work in their home communities at prevailing wages—but are herded off into camps where they perform manual labor on jobs of little social significance and without compensation. The men or the churches provide their maintenance at the rate of a dollar a day.

Not all the men, however, are kept permanently in the work camps; many are released to work in groups on special projects which afford maintenance, such as in hospitals and dairy farms. Here again, they are unpaid, and their dependents uncared for.

The regimented and unsatisfying nature of the plan has led several hundred men to refuse to accept it, and they have been imprisoned for their refusal, although under more liberal or flexible working arrangements, such as prevail in Britain, their scruples would not have been violated, and they would be usefully at work. The Civilian Public Service plan breaks down, therefore, in that a substantial group of men find it unacceptable and are forced into prison. This is the fault of administrative officials of the government, although some pacifists lay a share of the blame upon the churches, who, they say, by accepting the program offered prevented the development of a program acceptable to all.

Beyond this basic criticism of the program, these specific faults have been the subject of much dissatisfaction: the work is controlled by military officers on the staff of the Director of Selective Service who do not allow the church agencies sufficient responsibility; the men are not paid nor their dependents cared for; the work projects are seldom of any real social significance or capable of employing the talents of the men; projects which would afford maintenance should more rapidly replace those which do not; strict discipline, regimentation and inflexibility characterize the administration of the work.

Against this must be set the fact that many of the men find the present arrangements tolerable, and some of the work accomplished has real value, as the staffing of mental hospitals and the fighting of fires by parachutists.

Criticism of Selective Service officials for their failure to respond to the need for adjustment, growth and improvement culminated in a delegation to President

Roosevelt comprising Rufus Jones, the Quaker leader; Bishop Wm. Appleton Lawrence of the Episcopal Church, and Ernest Angell, New York lawyer, all representing the National Committee on Conscientious Objectors of the American Civil Liberties Union. After hearing their criticisms in detail, the President referred the matter to subordinates for further study, and an executive order was prepared for his signature which would transfer jurisdiction of the work of conscientious objectors to the Department of the Interior, which had already shown itself free from many of the objectionable attitudes of the army officers who have had control. This order was never signed, because of the strong opposition put up by Selective Service officials, who failed, however, to answer the basic criticisms. The position of the Committee is well put in the following letter to the President from one of its most prominent members:

July 17, 1944.

Hon. Franklin D. Roosevelt,
The White House,
Washington, D. C.

Dear Mr. President:

I wish to thank you for your letter of June 23rd.

What perturbs our Committee is the fact that for the first time in the history of the United States there has been brought into being a system of internment camps at which forced labor without pay is exacted by the government as the price for being allowed to hold a religious belief.

No words of the Selective Training and Service Act direct that internment camps be created, nor does the statute deny that the laborer, even though a conscientious objector, is worthy of his hire. These devices have been created by administrative orders. Most disturbing, they penalize the innocent dependents of the internees, including women and children for whom no provision whatever is made.

Under the statute, these problems could be solved by assigning the conscientious objector to work of national importance where the work already exists—as in hospitals, schools, community services, etc.—and allowing him to receive the prevailing wage, providing it is no higher than army pay. The language of the statute does not require punishment of the objector for his religious belief by payless work and by internment in segregated camps, but simply that he be "assigned" to work of national importance under rules and regulations devised by the President.

It is because the present system represents a serious blow to religious liberty and is promulgated in your name, that I feel you will wish to give further attention to this problem.

Respectfully yours,
HARRY EMERSON FOSDICK.

So much for Civilian Public Service as it now is, but what of the future?

As the war draws toward a close it becomes increasingly possible that we shall have some form of conscription with us in peace-time. England and the United States are the last of modern industrial nations to escape conscription as a permanent institution. Although the ability of our nation to withstand a long conflict may perhaps be ascribed to our not having wasted ourselves in military preparations, it looks as though we are on the verge of a revolutionary change in foreign policy which will bring us politically into international affairs which have long been only an economic concern, armed with a vast military establishment for the policing of the post-war world. This will be held to justify conscription, which has already been offered to Congress by Representative May, Chairman of the House Committee on Military Affairs.

It is not only possible that we shall have conscription, but also that the present form of it will not come to an end, but will simply be transmuted into a program for permanent training of eighteen-year-olds. If this is so, Selective Service as we now know it will be the model on which permanent conscription will be built, and doubtless the exemptions for conscience will be shaped in part by the war experience.

As the question became imminent, there was put forward by some of those active in Civilian Public Service the suggestion that pacifists should propose to Congress the sort of plan for conscientious objectors which they would like to see enacted into the law, drawing on the past performance of the Civilian Public Service program. Apparently these people intended to propose methods by which compulsory service for conscientious objectors could be made to work in peace-time.

I would as soon propose to the devil how he should operate an establishment in the nether regions. For it seems to me that while some pacifists may have condoned conscription of conscience under the duress of war, it is altogether wrong for them to have anything to do with such compulsion in time of peace. Pacifists stand for peace, for freedom of conscience, for the importance of the individual, and the dignity of his soul.

Yet all these things are destroyed when a year or more of a man's life is conscripted by the state. Service to one's country when voluntary is a noble thing, when compulsory is degrading, and when in violation of conscience is immoral.

Happily, the good sense of most pacifists will not allow them, I believe, to be persuaded into a perpetuation of Civilian Public Service in peace-time or the condoning of any sort of compulsory service. A wide expression of opinion among the Civilian Public Service men themselves indicates that they are heartily opposed to the making of any representations to Congress regarding compulsory service, but favor only complete opposition to post-war conscription as such. This is not true, however, of the Mennonites and Brethren, who do not oppose conscription so long as they are exempted from military service.

Once that post-war conscription becomes inevitable, if that is to be, then conscientious objectors will have to be provided for in some way, even if it is by the building of more prisons. When that time comes, the temptation to continue the status quo, that is to say Civilian Public Service, will be strong, but for the reasons I have given, that temptation should be overcome, as many pacifists will not accept compulsory service of any sort as a permanent thing.

What sort of a program should be adopted? There is no one answer to this question; many schemes might work and fairly well. Only one requirement is essential, that the program must be voluntary in character, perhaps within certain prescribed fields of work, so that those who insist on freedom of conscience will be enabled to follow their conscience in choosing the way in which they will serve the state.

Under a voluntary program, significant service will surely emerge. Many men will give their labor voluntarily to the state, whereas they would work heartlessly under compulsion or would refuse to work and would have to be maintained in prison. For when did the slave or conscript compare with the free man in the value of his production? The pacifist churches and organizations will come forward gladly, no doubt, to assist in providing significant work for those young men who are unwilling to train themselves for war. There is much to be done, and conscientious objectors are anxious to begin rebuilding instead of merely resisting the trend to destruction.

Chapter 2

The Religious Test of Conscientious Objection

THE NARROWNESS of the Selective Training and Service Act with respect to the requirement of a religious source for conscientious objection continues to present a most difficult and painful problem. There are now in prison perhaps three or four hundred conscientious objectors who are unquestionably sincere in their scruples against war but who do not fall within the term "religious" as it has been interpreted by the draft boards and the courts. Very few of these men have been released on parole, despite the obvious injustice of imprisoning sincere conscientious objectors as though they were genuine criminals, merely because inadequate consideration by Congress and narrowness of administrative construction of the law has resulted in an exemption for conscience which is not nearly so broad as it should be. These men are legally and technically guilty of crime, but certainly not criminals in a social or moral sense.

Even after the decisions by the Circuit Court of Appeals in New York in the *Kauten* and *Phillips* cases,* holding that objection derived from conscience, as distinguished from personal or political objection, is religious in nature, draft boards and hearing officers con-

* 103 Federal Reporter, 2nd Series, 703; and 135 Id. 521; see pages 11-18 and 51-62 of "The Conscientious Objector and the Law."

tinued to construe narrowly the religious test of exemption and have excluded therefrom many conscientious objectors who were religious in a broad sense, but were unable to demonstrate church membership and attachment to the formal concepts of theology.

An outstanding example of this attitude is found in one of the three hearing officers for New York City, Jackson A. Dykman, prominent Brooklyn lawyer and President of the New York State Bar Association, who has openly refused to follow the *Kauten* and *Phillips* decisions. Mr. Dykman recommended denial of exemption as a conscientious objector for a member of the Ethical Culture Society on the sole ground that he did not profess belief in a deity, although the Ethical Culture Society is commonly recognized as a religious group, is exempt from taxation as a religious society and its leaders are empowered by law to solemnize marriages. In another case still more striking, Mr. Dykman recommended denial of exemption for a man who subscribed to Christianity and the teachings of Jesus, but did not join a church until 1942, and then did so primarily for social reasons. The hearing officer found that this man was unquestionably a pacifist and completely credible, but lacked any basis in religious training or belief because he had failed to attend church for about nine years and then joined a church primarily for social reasons. The hearing officer gave full credit to the registrant's testimony that he was a Christian pacifist, yet denied him exemption *solely because he had not expressed his Christianity through membership in a church.*

In all fairness it must be said that Mr. Dykman is a good and conscientious hearing officer in other respects, although this cannot be said of some hearing officers, who have exhibited at times both bigotry and incompetence. It may be of interest in passing to note that Mr. Dykman, a prominent lay member of the Episcopal Church, was reported in the New York *Times* of October 12, 1943, to have proposed at a convention of the church a resolution prohibiting its Commission on Conscientious Objectors from raising funds to support its conscientious objectors.

The recommendations of the hearing officers are reviewed by the Department of Justice in Washington as a matter of routine. Such flagrant decisions as those mentioned have been allowed to pass by and therefore the Department of Justice must share the responsibility for this narrow interpretation of the law.

The final authority, however, for interpreting the law rests with the Director of Selective Service, General Lewis B. Hershey, since he has been entrusted by the President with the responsibility for deciding Presidential appeals. For a long time General Hershey persisted in the view that belief in a deity was necessary for exemption, despite the *Kauten* decision which is plainly to the contrary. However, in the case of the member of the Ethical Culture Society mentioned above, General Hershey reversed the decision of Mr. Dykman and granted exemption, thereby indicating that he has changed his position and now supports the rule laid down in the *Kauten* decision. In the other case, however, General Hershey refused to intervene, and this man is now in prison.

also said that such an objection 'may justly be regarded as a response of the individual to an inward mentor, call it conscience or God, that is for many persons at the present time the equivalent of what has always been thought a religious impulse."

It appears therefore that the first round in the struggle for a liberal exemption for conscience has been won, as the Department of Justice and the Director of Selective Service both adhere to the principles of the *Kauten* case. However, the struggle is not yet finished, since not all draft boards and courts will follow the *Kauten* case, and also because political objectors are still unprovided for, as are those who ask total exemption, granted to about six per cent. of British objectors, but granted to none by our Congress.

If, as seems quite possible, conscription is to remain with us after the war, there will surely be strong representations made to Congress for the elimination of the religious basis for exemption.

There appears to be no sound reason why a sincere conscientious objector who bases his objection, for example, upon the principles of socialism or vegetarianism, or even refusal to kill members of his own nation or race, should not receive equal consideration with the man who can demonstrate religious grounds for his opposition to war.

The British draft law imposes no religious or other requirement for exemption. The British Appellate Tribunal has even granted exemption to an Indian nationalist who had no objection to war as such, but was unwilling to fight for the British Empire so long as

India was not free.* This case was argued by Fenner Brockway, Chairman of the Central Board for Conscientious Objectors, who stated that a political objection should be regarded as within the statute when so deeply held that it became a matter of inner conviction as to right or wrong, and not just a matter of opinion. This reasoning was apparently adopted by the Tribunal. If our laws were changed to conform to the British practice, we would exempt all conscientious objectors whether religious, political or otherwise who could demonstrate that their opposition was based upon an inner conviction of right or wrong, and not upon mere opinion, or personal opposition to military service.

In other words, the proper test of conscientious objection is not the test of religious training and belief, or any other similar test, all of which must prove too narrow since the motives of human behavior are unlimited in scope. The only proper test is simply whether the opposition to war is based upon principle, whether moral, humanitarian or religious, and not on mere opinion or personal expediency.

---

* The case of Suresh Vaidya discussed in the May, 1944, issue of the Bulletin of the Central Board for Conscientious Objectors, London, England.

Chapter 3

Prison and Parole

THE SITUATION with regard to prison sentences remains unchanged. The average sentence imposed upon conscientious objectors is 30.6 months, although the average sentence for all Federal prisoners is only 22.1 months.*

There are nearly three thousand conscientious objectors in prison, about two-thirds of whom are Jehovah's Witnesses. The members of this sect are in prison because they have failed to gain exemption as ministers, and because the law does not provide total exemption for those who refuse any service whatever.

The shocking number of men who are now imprisoned for conscience's sake in this country is emphasized by comparison with the situation in Great Britain where only about 200 conscientious objectors are now in prison out of 57,000 whose claims have been heard by the draft tribunals.† This means that *fifteen times* as many conscientious objectors are in prison in the United States as in Britain, although there are probably fewer conscientious objectors in this country. The small number of conscientious objectors in British prisons is due principally to the fact that sentences are very short,

---

* From the annual report of the Bureau of Prisons for the year ending June 30, 1943. Sentenced less severely than C.O's. are violators of narcotic laws—20.8 months, liquor laws—10.6 months, white slave laws—28.3 months, and postal laws—27.3 months.

† P. 29, Aug., 1944, Bulletin of Central Board for Conscientious Objectors, London.

frequently a fine or a few weeks imprisonment, and prison sentences for more than six months are rare.

It is a startling fact that conscientious objectors make up about one-sixth of the entire Federal prison population.* In some prisons, such as the prison at Danbury, Connecticut, more than half the inmates are conscientious objectors. Furthermore, conscientious objectors account for two-thirds of the men in prison for Selective Service violations.

The prisoners fall into several categories, including those who refused to register, refused to accept service in the work camps, or refused to be inducted after failing to gain exemption. The last official figures of July 1, 1944, showed that of 4,363 objectors then convicted, 2,596 refused induction, 1,365 refused work camps, 258 would not register, and 144 violated other provisions.†

It is apparent, therefore, that the problem of conscientious objectors is one of the biggest problems confronting the Department of Justice, more particularly the United States Attorneys, the Bureau of Prisons and the Board of Parole. If the law were more liberally applied, the problem would be much less, and this is a strong practical reason for greater liberality.

It must be recorded that the handling of prison and parole problems has not been characterized by humanity or intelligence. There has been no real attempt to solve these problems in decent fashion, the chief aim of prison officials being to avoid public criticism which they

---

* The Bureau of Prisons reports 18,392 prisoners on June 30, 1944, of whom 3,223 are CO's.
† Annual report of the Department of Justice for the year ending June 30, 1944.

imagine might result from leniency toward conscientious objectors. This fear of public criticism, responsible for much bad treatment of C.O.'s., may well be groundless. A survey of public opinion by Dr. Leo P. Crespi of Princeton University shows little intolerance; for instance, 93 per cent. of those questioned thought that C.O.'s. should be maintained and paid by the government. See also the Canadian experience mentioned at page 60.

The initial mistake was in treating conscientious objectors as ordinary criminals. United States Attorneys, following a policy which holds throughout the Department of Justice, have consistently recommended heavy prison sentences for conscientious objectors and have uniformly opposed suspended sentences and probation. For the most part trial judges have acceded to the demands of the Department of Justice and have imposed heavy sentences, averaging about three years, although sentences imposed for like offenses in England range from a few pounds fine to imprisonment of a few months, the maximum sentence permitted by the law being imprisonment for two years.

However, in a few instances judges have been sufficiently liberal and courageous to suspend sentence and allow a conscientious objector to remain free upon probation. The conditions of probation are discretionary with the judge. In a recent case in New York City the senior judge of the District Court, John C. Knox, suspended the sentence of a conscientious objector, requiring him to work as an orderly in a hospital at not exceeding $50 a month, which is equal to basic pay in the armed forces. Similarly, Judge Carroll C. Hincks in Connecticut granted probation to an architect, allowing him to work for an architectural firm at $50 per month. There have been very few such cases in the East, although the District Court at Los Angeles, California, has made several similar dispositions permitting conscientious objectors to work on farms and in other work of public importance.

An immediate and wholesale solution to the entire prison problem would be accomplished if the Department of Justice would take the attitude that these men do not belong in prison and should be placed upon probation. This could be done without the consent of Selective Service officials, which is required for parole. It would save the Bureau of Prisons many headaches and would save the taxpayers a very substantial outlay. The maintenance of 3,000 conscientious objectors at the rate of $771 per man per year* is costing the taxpayers over $2,000,000 per year. The costs for the entire war are staggering. Assuming that 4,500 conscientious objectors will pass through the prisons, a figure which we are already approaching, and will stay there for two years on the average (allowing for deductions for good behavior and paroles), the cost to the nation will amount to about $7,000,000. Not only will this sum

---

* This is the average cost of maintaining prisoners at the nine institutions to which conscientious objectors are mostly sent, namely Ashland, Ky.; Danbury, Conn.; Lewisburg, Pa.; MacNeil Island, Wash.; Milan, Mich.; Petersburg, Va.; Sandstone, Minn.; Texarkana, Tex., and Tucson, Ariz., as shown in the "Directory of Correctional Institutions in the United States and Canada" of the American Prison Association. New York, 1944.

have been needlessly spent, but these men might have produced many times that amount in the value of their labor, so contributing to relieve the drastic shortage of manpower. Keeping these men in prison is a luxury which we can ill afford.

A second possible solution to this problem is afforded by the procedure for parole of persons who no longer require rehabilitation in prison. It seems quite obvious that true conscientious objectors cannot be reformed by imprisonment and that no useful purpose is served either to them or to society, unless it be the purpose of revenge.

The possible reasons for imprisonment are (1) retribution, (2) protection of society, (3) the deterrent effect on others, and (4) rehabilitation of the prisoner.

Although the desire for retribution is a normal human reaction to crime, this is not regarded as a proper moral basis for punishment and penologists endeavor to eliminate the element of revenge in the treatment of prisoners.

Society needs no protection from conscientious objectors, since they are generally law-abiding citizens except for this one aberration. At most it can be said that they should be required to engage in some activity comparable to military service, in order to share the country's burdens and so that the feelings of families of men in the armed forces will not be outraged.

Similarly the imprisonment of conscientious objectors has little deterrent effect upon others, since their refusal of military service is based upon principle and not upon fear of consequences. Although some will accept military service rather than imprisonment, they will surely be poor soldiers.

This brings us to the last basis for punishment, rehabilitation of the prisoner, as the only basis which applies to conscientious objectors. Yet here also it is obvious that rehabilitation is either hopeless or unnecessary, since no amount of imprisonment will alter a conviction which is based upon inward scruples and in all other respects these men need no rehabilitation. In fact they are usually able, intelligent and moral individuals.

There is only one reason, therefore, for keeping these men in prison and that is the reason of revenge or retribution, which is hardly a proper reason for the Bureau of Prisons or for a civilized nation. Nothing could be more plain than that justice and morals require the elimination of conscientious objectors from the prison system. If judges will not suspend prison sentences, then the Bureau of Prisons and Selective Service should be quick to grant parole. However, paroles have been few and have been granted only after long delays.

Up to August 1, 1944, according to an unofficial survey,* 626 conscientious objectors applied for special parole under Executive Order 8641. Of these, 153 have been granted parole, 212 were refused parole (151 by the Bureau of Prisons and 61 by Selective Service, which must both concur) and the balance are pending. Only 33 men so paroled were allowed to take up jobs, the

---

* These figures were compiled by the National Service Board for Religious Objectors and the National Committee on Conscientious Objectors.

other 120 being sent to Civilian Public Service Camps. In addition to the special parole, ordinary parole is available to conscientious objectors, as it is to all prisoners, at the end of one-third of the sentence. Ordinary parole has been given to 180 conscientious objectors, but instead of being allowed to return home to any proper job, like all other offenders, the conscientious objectors are restricted to jobs in hospitals and other "public service" projects at least 150 miles from their homes at wages not exceeding $50 per month, plus maintenance.

Thus conscientious objectors are treated much more strictly than ordinary criminals in regard to parole. Only about one-fourth of their parole applications have been granted, and many more do not apply because the terms of parole are so limited, whereas 44.8 per cent. of all parole applications are granted, as shown by the annual report of the Bureau of Prisons for the year ending June 30, 1943.

The provisions with regard to special parole were radically changed on April 15, 1944, in a joint memorandum issued by the Department of Justice and Selective Service headquarters, which, however, has not been made a part of the Selective Service regulations. The new procedure provides that all Selective Service violators who have served sixty days are to be reclassified by draft boards attached to the prisons into I-A, I-A-O, or IV-E, and then given the usual pre-induction physical examination, at which their prison status is not revealed. Before being given the physical examination, the prisoner will be asked whether he will agree to accept the service for which he has been reclassified. If he agrees to accept such service (for instance, if a man reclassified by the prison draft board from I-A to IV-E agrees to accept CPS service) and passes the physical examination, he may be paroled to the service for which he is assigned; but if he fails the physical examination, he will be classified in IV-F and may be given general parole. This should mean that he will return to his home and seek gainful employment of his choice, but a later memorandum provides that IV-F men are to be released only to hospitals and similar jobs at nominal wages.

If the prisoner has refused to accept the service for which he is classified and passes the physical examination, he will again be given an opportunity to accept such service, and if he still refuses, he will thereafter be eligible only for the one-third-of-term parole. If a man who has refused to accept the service for which classified fails the examination, he will likewise be eligible only for the one-third-of-term parole.

The new procedure, although hailed with joy by conscientious objectors, has been so far a dismal failure, apparently because the Bureau of Prisons is still insisting upon rigorous conditions for parole, conditions which most prisoners are unwilling to accept.

Not only have the Bureau of Prisons and Selective Service authorities been rigid and uncompromising in their attitude toward paroles, but the parole board itself has exhibited some amazing tendencies. Not only has the board treated conscientious objectors more harshly than ordinary criminals, but it has indulged in wholesale violation of civil liberties. The Jehovah's Witnesses are concerned principally in preaching their faith and are such zealous religionists that they will suffer long imprisonment rather than give up the right to preach. Nevertheless the parole board has refused to parole Jehovah's Witnesses unless they will agree while on parole to refrain from their religious activities. This plainly interferes with the religious liberty guaranteed by the First Amendment to the United States Constitution. This represents religious persecution no less severe than that which forced our forefathers to emigrate from Europe. This is the sort of tyrannical disregard for human liberty which the world is still fighting to eradicate. Yet we find such tyranny in the United States Board of Parole, which is denying reiligous liberty to over 2,000 Jehovah's Witnesses.

Imprisonment of conscientious objectors in this war is not only marked by disregard of civil liberties and ordinary decency, but will go down in history as indicating the incompetence and stupidity of our government, which has failed to solve the simple problem of removing from prison 3,000 conscientious objectors who never should have been sent there, and who now comprise one-sixth of the entire Federal prison population and are maintained at the cost of millions of dollars a year. The problem has been solved in our sister democracies of England and Canada; in the former there are only about 200 conscientious objectors in prison and in the latter fewer still. Perhaps the difference between their governments and ours lies in this: the British and Canadians treat conscientious objectors as human beings, albeit somewhat eccentric but nevertheless entitled to respect, while our government treats them as unpatriotic slackers who should be punished for their views.

There are some further developments to report in the well-known case of brutalities inflicted upon Stanley Murphy and Louis Taylor at the medical center for Federal prisoners at Springfield, Missouri. Despite censorship and official secrecy, it has been pretty well established that the men were brutally beaten on numerous occasions and that Murphy was confined naked in a bare tiled cell while Taylor was kept in a ward with violently insane patients.

The Director of the Bureau of Prisons, James V. Bennett, never made public the report of the investigation which was conducted regarding the alleged atrocities. In particular the report of Austin MacCormack, prominent penologist and head of the Osborne Association, was suppressed although it is believed that the report was highly critical of the conduct of the warden and other prison officials. At least one good result has come in the removal of Dr. Cox as warden of the institution. He has been replaced by a Dr. Pescor, who is reported to be a sympathetic and conscientious official. Nevertheless, Murphy and Taylor are still confined at Springfield.

Because of continued public outcry and demands for a real investigation, Mr. Bennett finally was forced to order a second investigation which he conducted himself, although he permitted two reporters from Missouri newspapers to attend the investigative sessions. That a public official whose department is under criticism should himself conduct an investigation concerning his actions and his subordinates is an effrontery to the good sense of the public. As might have been expected, Mr. Bennett's investigation produced nothing but a "whitewash." Meanwhile, many concerned people, including Norman Thomas, Socialist candidate for President, have continued to press for a Congressional investigation.

Although long prevented by inability to obtain counsel with the meager funds at its command, the National Committee on Conscientious Objectors of the American Civil Liberties Union has finally secured capable and experienced attorneys who are acting without fee and will file suits on behalf Murphy and Taylor for $7,500 damages against James V. Bennett, Director of the Bureau of Prisons; and Dr. Ora H. Cox, former warden at Springfield. At the same time they will seek to prevent further mistreatment by a habeas corpus proceeding.* Since administrative processes have been unavailing, only by these means can relief be obtained and an impartial investigation assured.

---

* The recent case of *Coffin* v. *Reichard*, 143 Fed. 2nd 443, holds that habeas corpus may be used to correct maltreatment of a prisoner even where his release is not sought.

Chapter 4

Cat and Mouse

REPEATED PROSECUTIONS for virtually the same offense have taken place in a number of cases involving those who refused to register, although in the case of other violations second prosecutions are usually prevented by action of the draft boards, which have been set up attached to each of the Federal prisons, and which generally classify a prisoner who has completed his sentence in Class IV-F. Out of 2,292 convictions in the year ending July 1, 1944, only 55 were for a second offense, and one for a third.*

The problem in England has proved to be a much greater one than in the United States. Repeated prosecutions have taken place in a large number of cases.

Notable among these is the case of George Elphick, who was exempted as a conscientious objector but ordered to register for civilian defense duties commonly known as "fire-watch." This was contrary to his conscientious scruples and he refused to obey. In response to a summons, he pleaded guilty at Police Court in December, 1941, and served twenty-eight days in prison upon his refusal to pay a £5 fine. Within a month after his release he was prosecuted a second time and then fined a like amount, although this time the fine was paid by a friend. Two weeks later he received a third order

---

* Annual report of Department of Justice.

to report for "fire-watch" and again spent four weeks in prison in lieu of payment of a fine. In December, 1942, Elphick received a fourth order directing him to "fire-watch" which he again refused. Again he was sentenced but refused to pay his fine and spent the Christmas holidays in prison.

By this time the case was attracting national attention, which even reached the floor of the House of Lords. Prosecution, however, rested with the local Borough Council, which seem immune to outside criticism. Accordingly a fifth prosecution was undertaken and this time two months' imprisonment was imposed without the alternative of a fine. This provoked questioning in the House of Commons directed at the Home Secretary, Mr. Herbert Morrison. A sixth prosecution was nevertheless instituted, but withdrawn because of a technical defect, to be followed soon after by a seventh prosecution, which collapsed when it was pointed out in court that the Borough Council's authorization to prosecute was made before Elphick had violated the order directing him to "fire-watch." The Council was apparently so eager that they began to prosecute before the offense had been committed.

In January, 1944, an eighth prosecution resulted in a £10 fine or two months in prison. After Elphick had served a month of this term the balance of the fine was paid by a friend.

When the ninth prosecution was begun it looked as though the Borough officials were indefatigable, and would continue to prosecute so long as the offense should remain on the statute books. But with many eyes throughout the country focused upon their proceedings, and in the face of the express disapproval of the Minister of Home Security, who is in charge of the entire administration of fire watching, the magistrates who heard the ninth prosecution of George Elphick decided to temper justice with common sense, if not with mercy. At the close of the hearing their Chairman made this statement:

"This is the ninth time Elphick has appeared before us, and I say again, as I have said on every previous occasion, that the Bench entirely disagree with his attitude, and we fail to understand it. We realize that the case is an extremely difficult one, but we want to make it quite clear that we entirely disagree with his actions and we think he would be better advised to follow the example of his many friends who have taken the opportunity of doing fire-watching. Having said that, we do feel that his case has been before us quite often enough, and we cannot see any useful purpose is served by further prosecution. It is quite clear that the object of prosecuting in all these cases, as has been pointed out by the Home Secretary, is to ensure that duty is carried out. The main object is to bring people to a better frame of mind and to secure their willing co-operation, but we confess we have failed to bring Elphick to a better frame of mind, and we regret that. The question is whether it is worth while to go on trying. The law cannot make a man do things—it can only punish him for not doing them. The proceedings at St. Albans have been quoted, and it seems a somewhat similar case. We are rather impressed by that and we propose to follow their example and impose a fine of £1."*

* As quoted in August, 1944. Bulletin of the Central Board for Conscientious Objectors, London.

Elphick paid his fine and departed, happy no doubt in the knowledge that he had at last convinced his judges that his conscience, obedient to a law higher than that by which he was judged, could not be overcome by punishment of man's devising.

We have fortunately been spared such spectacles in the United States, but this should give us small cause for rejoicing, since the principal reason is that sentences in this country average about three years, while in England sentences are rarely more than a few months.

Chapter 5

Constitutional Questions

SEVERAL CASES have been instituted in the courts attacking the constitutionality of the Selective Training and Service Act and the regulations with regard to the Civilian Public Service system imposed upon conscientious objectors.

The best prepared of these cases is the case of R. Boland Brooks, who was at one time connected with the National Service Board for Religious Objectors and later was in charge of the Washington office of the National Committee on Conscientious Objectors. Brooks is a New York lawyer who has been active in pacifist circles. He was classified in IV-E and ordered to report to the government operated camp at Mancos, Colorado, which he refused to do.

Upon being indicted, Brooks filed a demurrer and plea in abatement through his attorney, Ernest Angell, Chairman of the National Committee on Conscientious Objectors, in which it was contended: (1) The administrative regulations of the Selective Service System establishing and prescribing the operation of the civilian work camps for conscientious objectors exceed the powers delegated to the President by the Selective Service Act and by the President to the Director of the Selective Service System; (2) The Constitution has not delegated to Congress any power to draft civilian labor for non-defense, non-military purposes; (3) The statute and the regulations violate the due process clause of the Fifth Amendment and the free exercise of religion guaranteed by the First Amendment; (4) The statute and the regulations violate the Thirteenth Amendment in that the compulsory labor required of the conscientious objectors assigned to the camps, coupled with their enforced detention therein for the duration of the war and six months thereafter, constitute involuntary servitude.

All of Brooks' contentions were overruled by Judge Rifkind, who wrote:*

"In keeping with historical precedent, Congress has extended to conscientious objectors exemption from combatant service, and for the first time has gone beyond that and given immunity to those whose scruples forbit participation in non-combatant military service. It has not, however, exempted those who are conscientiously opposed to 'compulsory labor in civilian camps' from compliance with the requirement of the statute that they 'be assigned to work of national importance under civilian direction.'

"In so doing Congress has not violated the First Amendment. Even the minority opinion in *United States* v. *Macintosh*, 1931, 283 U. S. 605, 633, 51 S. Ct. 570, 578, 75 L. Ed. 1302 said: 'I agree with the statement in the opinion of the Circuit Court of Appeals in the present case that: 'This federal legislation is indicative of the actual operation of the principles of the Constitution, that a person with conscientious or religious scruples need not bear arms, although, as a member of society, he may be obliged to render services of a noncombatant nature'.'"

---

* *U. S.* v. *Brooks,* 54 Fed. Supp. 995, Apr. 20, 1944.

"I conclude that the Act and the Regulations do not violate the First Amendment.

"Nor do they violate the Thirteenth. The asserted incompatibility of the Act and Regulations with the Thirteenth Amendment is predicated on the treatment by the defendant of the provision for work of national importance as completely severed and independent from the comprehensive mobilization contemplated by the Selective Training and Service Act. To attack these regulations as if they constituted a discrete measure for the exaction of labor from persons holding specified beliefs is to attack a straw man. The regulations, as well as the statutory provision for work of national importance, must be construed, as indeed they are, as part of a comprehensive scheme for the utilization of the able-bodied manpower of the nation for its defense. The argument advanced by the defendant leads to this anomaly: That Congress may, without doing violence to the Constitution, compel the induction of conscientious objectors into the armed forces, but that if Congress chooses to honor their scruples of conscience it must forego their services altogether. I do not believe that the Thirteenth Amendment can be validly charged with introducing so inflexible a rule.

"The first constitution of New York, adopted in 1777, provided: 'That all such of the inhabitants of this State being of the people called Quakers as, from scruples of conscience may be averse to the bearing of arms, be therefrom excused by the legislature; and do pay to the State such sums of money, in lieu of their personal service, as the same may, in the judgment of the legislature be worth.' Art. 40, *United States* v. *Macintosh*, 1931, 283 U. S. 605, 632, 51 S. Ct. 570, 75 L. Ed. 1302. Would it be sensible to test the validity of such a provision, in the light of present constitutional requirements, by treating it as a tax imposed upon Quakers *qua* Quakers? Could it be argued, after the adoption of the Fourteenth Amendment that the collection of such sums of money from a conscientious objector constituted a taking of property without due process of law or a denial of the equal protection of the laws?

"Assignment of a conscientious objector to service does not constitute the imposition of an invalid condition upon a privilege. *Western Union T. Co.* v. *Kansas,* 1909, 216 U. S. 1, 30 S. Ct. 190, 54 L. Ed. 355. The exaction of service from conscientious objectors under civilian direction is not a condition upon exemption from induction into the armed forces. The assignment to work of national importance is not predicated upon the voluntary assent of the conscientious objector any more than the induction of other citizens in the armed forces is premised upon their consent. Both legislative mandates flow from the same constitutional power. The fact that the former work under civilian direction is quite irrelevant. I find nothing in the Constitution which requires that training for defense shall be conducted by military rather than by civilian officers. Nor does it matter that the actual labor performed by the assignees is not directly in aid of the defense of the United States or of its military establishment. It is sufficient that in the judgment of Congress such labor is of national importance; that its performance by assignees releases others for services more directly concerned with military action; and that assignment of conscientious objectors tends to deter others from asserting a claim to exemption.

"I conclude that neither the Act nor the Regulations trespass upon the Thirteenth Amendment.

"The argument that the conditions of service in the civilian camps as imposed by the regulations are so discriminatory in comparison with conditions at military camps as to amount to a denial of due process is quite without merit. True, the assignee's pay is less, he cannot buy insurance on the same terms, he receives no dependency allowance nor compensation for injury. These privileges and benefits are clearly matters of legislative discretion. It cannot be said as a matter of law that service in the armed forces, together with its attendant perils, is so comparable to the peaceful pursuits of a civilian camp that the withholding from the latter of benefits accorded to the former amounts to a denial of due process.

"That the statute itself contains no unconstitutional delegation of legislative power, Const. Art. 1, Sec. 1, is apparent from a reading of Sec. 310 (a) which simply provides, 'The President is authorized—(1) to prescribe the necessary rules and regulations to carry out the provisions of the Act; * * *'

"But the defendant urges that the regulations exceed the powers delegated by Congress in the following respect:

"(a) quasi-penal detention in isolated internment camps, called euphemistically 'civilian public service camps,'

"(b) labor without pay ($3 per month 'cash allowances'),

"(c) no element of choice of type of service or location,

"(d) labor-internment for six months beyond the duration of the war,

"(e) power of officials arbitrarily to assess fines, to deny furloughs, to add 40 days of service annually to the total term—all without hearing or appeal,

"(f) no provision for dependent's allowances, death or disability benefits.

"Of these, items (d) and (e) are not now in issue. It will be time enough when and if these powers are exercised to pass upon their validity. Item (f) is a matter of congressional action and since Congress has not authorized dependency allowances or disability benefits for camp assignees the regulations cannot be said to exceed the authority wher they make no provision therefor. Attempts to obtain such legislation have been made and failed. Sec. S. 315 and S. 675, First Session, 78th Congress. Item (c) does not exceed the power conferred by statute, since the statute nowhere suggests that the assignee shall have a choice of work or location. Items (a) and (b) deal with the type of camp organization and the rate of pay. True, the statute says nothing about camps nor does it prescribe the rate of compensation; but that Congress has knowledge of the system of camps and has, within appropriate limits, lodged discretion concerning the rate of compensation, is clear from the appropriation acts and the hearings held in connection therewith. Thus, the Act of June 27, 1942, Public Law 630, 56 Stat. 416, appropriating funds for the Selective Service System for the fiscal year 1943, provides as follows: ' * * * That such amounts as may be necessary shall be available for the planning, directing, and operation of a program of work of national importance under civilian direction, either independently or in cooperation with governmental or non-governmental agencies, and the assignment and delivery thereto of individuals found to be conscientiously opposed to participation in work of the land or naval forces, which cooperation with other agencies may include the furnishing of funds to and acceptance of money, services, or other forms of assistance from such non-governmental agencies for the more effectual accomplishment of the work; and including also the pay and allowances of such individuals at rates not in excess of those paid to persons inducted into the Army, under the Selective Service System and such privileges as are accorded such inductees: * * * '

"I conclude that the plaintiff's demurrer to the plea in abatement must be sustained and that defendant's demurrer to the indictment must be overruled."

Brooks was sentenced to three years' imprisonment and has filed an appeal. He will also face disbarment proceedings which will raise the question of whether a conscientious objector should be disbarred. Several conscientious objectors have been disbarred in New

York under similar circumstances, but none of them has put up any opposition. While the New York statute makes disbarment for a felony conviction automatic, there are cases which hold that a federal felony which is not a felony under New York law does not require disbarment and that the court in such cases has discretion whether or not to order disbarment.

As post-war conscription becomes a real possibility and as the end of the war approaches, the constitutionality of such legislation becomes an important question. However, it may be that public opinion in favor of post-war conscription will be so strong that constitutional considerations will be ignored by Congress. Nevertheless, it should be pointed out that any program of permanent peace-time conscription would deeply infringe the civil liberties of every male citizen of military age. While the liberties guaranteed by the constitution are not unlimited, it is hard to believe that the necessity for military preparedness justifies such extreme inroads upon personal freedom.

Chapter 6

Involuntary Servitude

WHILE I HAVE NOT changed the view which I expressed in *The Conscientious Objector and the Law,* that service to the State is not "involuntary servitude" in violation of the Thirteenth Amendment, and while the courts have uniformly borne me out in this,* my view has been strongly criticized in several quarters by those who hold that enforced labor of conscientious objectors without compensation is a violation of the Thirteenth Amendment.

In order that the reader may have both sides of this question I give here the statement of R. Boland Brooks contained in his review of my book, published in "The Conscientious Objector" for November, 1943:

"On the question of involuntary servitude Mr. Cornell states. 'Nevertheless, it is clear that such work, although involuntary, would not be held by the Courts to be a violation of the 13th Amendment.' There is no final authority for this statement, nor does Mr. Cornell quote one.

"His argument that compulsory road service of six days a year and jury duty are controlling precedents for labor conscription without compensation, is, in my opinion,

---

* *United States* v. *Gormly,* 136 Fed. Rep., 2nd Series, 227, Certiorari denied 320 U. S., 753; *United States* v. *Mroz,* 136 Fed. Rep., 2nd Series, 221; *Weightman* v. *United States,* 142 Fed. Rep., 2nd Series, 188; *United States* v. *Brooks,* 54 Fed. Supp., 995; *Heflin* v. *Sanford,* 142 Fed. Rep., 2nd Series, 798. See also the opinion in the *Brooks* case, which is quoted above at page 32.

entirely unwarranted. This results, I believe, from his failure to distinguish between these brief incidents of the duties of citizenship, and complete control of human personality over relatively long periods of time. It is most unfortunate that Mr. Cornell should concede to the government a case of such vital importance which is still in process of being tested in the courts and needless to say he does not speak for the National Committee on Conscientious Objectors on the point."

While conscription of labor in lieu of military service may not be the sort of "servitude" intended by the 13th Amendment, there are other provisions of the Constitution which can be invoked with better reason. The entire Bill of Rights was intended to secure the citizen in his personal freedom, which is almost wholly lost to him under conscription.

Chapter 7

Military Control of Camps

MILITARY CONTROL of camps for conscientious objectors continues to be exercised by the army officers who comprise General Hershey's staff. This is one of the aspects of the Civilian Public Service system which is most objectionable to pacifists and which they have continually protested. The recent delegation to President Roosevelt from the National Committee on Conscientious Objectors made strong representations toward removal of the control of conscientious objectors from military officials.

The American Friends Service Committee, one of the bodies engaged in operating the camps, has asked for more complete control of the camps and is obviously somewhat unhappy over the present arrangements, but there is not yet any indication that such dissatisfaction will result in a change.

Since the law requires that conscientious objectors be assigned to work under civilian direction and control, the question as to whether the control exercised by army officers is illegal is continually being raised in the courts, but has been disposed of adversely in the cases that have thus far been decided, in most cases with but scant and unsympathetic consideration. Perhaps the appeal in the case of R. Boland Brooks referred to in Chapter 5 will produce a more careful consideration of this issue, since the Circuit Court of Appeals for the Second Circuit has most liberal and capable judges.

Chapter 8

Why C.O's. Are Not Paid

THERE IS NO CHANGE in the ruling of the Comptroller General that earnings of conscientious objectors may not be diverted to the support of their kind, but must go into the U. S. Treasury, but he has not yet, however, passed upon the question whether a conscientious objector may be permitted to retain wages earned by him. The previous arrangement continues whereby conscientious objectors engaged in work on farms and elsewhere at prevailing wages are not paid anything except for maintenance—not more than $15.00 per month—and the balance of their wages is deposited in a special fund in the Treasury. It has been estimated that $1,400,000 per year earned by conscientious objectors is withheld from them and deposited in this fund.*

Recently the Comptroller General has ruled that Selective Service officials may bring legal action against farmers who have failed to pay into the Treasury the earnings of C.O's. working on their farms. If this is done, the validity of the Comptroller General's rulings, which seem to rest on the premise that C.O's. are a species of slave whose labor belongs to the State, may be an issue, and judicial clarification of this matter may become possible.

Chief among the injustices which arise out of this

---

* "Information," weekly newsletter of C.P.S. Section of American Friends Service Committee, Philadelphia, Pa. Issue of Sept. 8, 1914.

situation is the unfortunate hardship on conscientious objectors having dependents.

In the case of the man who is willing to perform medical services in the armed forces, no problem is raised because he receives military pay and his family receives dependency allotments. But the conscientious objector who is classified in IV-E and assigned to a Civilian Public Service camp, since he receives no compensation whatever, often leaves a destitute family behind him. This is not only unjust, it is illegal, since the Selective Service regulations provide for the deferment of any man whose induction would result in extreme hardship to his dependents.

Despite the fact that extreme hardship is plainly involved by reason of the lack of pay or dependency allowances to conscientious objectors, men with families have been drafted into Civilian Public Service without regard to financial hardship. I am reliably informed that the Director of Selective Service has recognized the injustice of this, but because of his fear of public criticism has been unwilling to issue instructions to draft boards that they should defer impecunious conscientious objectors in order to prevent hardship to their families, although he has gone so far as to inform State directors of Selective Service that this problem requires attention. It is obvious, however, that in the absence of instructions, draft boards will continue to draft conscientious objectors despite financial hardship to their families. The boards are accustomed to disregard the financial question in drafting men into the armed forces and have not been told that a difference exists as to conscientious objectors.

A case involving this question is about to be taken into the Federal courts by the National Committee on Conscientious Objectors. This is the case of a conscientious objector who was assigned to a camp in Pennsylvania, although his wife was expecting a baby and was forced upon public relief after he was drafted. His release is being sought by means of a writ of habeas corpus. He argues that he was illegally denied a 3-D classification by his draft board, and assigned to camp, without regard to the extreme hardship to his family which would result.

It was for a time thought that Congress would remedy this situation by enacting a bill introduced by Representative Sparkman of Alabama, Chairman of the House Military Affairs Committee, which had the approval of both the House and Senate Committees, providing for support of dependents out of the earnings of conscientious objectors, which have been held in the Treasury. This bill required unanimous consent for its consideration. Such consent was prevented by the opposition of Representative Thomas of New Jersey and Brooks of Louisiana, who were also both members of the Military Affairs Committee. The debate on the measure as recorded in the Congressional Record* gives an interesting side-light on the attitudes of Congressmen on a problem affecting conscientious objectors.

"*The Clerk called the next bill, H. R. 3199, authorizing the appropriation of amounts received from the services of conscientious objectors for expenditure by the Selective Service System.*

---

* June 5, 1944, pp. 5420, 5421.

"The Speaker pro tempore: Is there objection to the present consideration of the bill?

"Mr. Thomas (N. J.): Mr. Speaker, reserving the right to object, I would like to ask the proponent of the bill some questions concerning this bill. . . . As I understand it, it has to do only with conscientious objectors?

"Mr. Sparkman: That is correct.

"Mr. Thomas: For the relief of dependent families of these conscientious objectors?

"Mr. Sparkman: For the relief of needy dependents.

"Mr. Thomas: How many conscientious objectors are there in the United States today?

"Mr. Sparkman: On the first of May of this year there were 6,985.

"Mr. Thomas: How many of these have needy dependents?

"Mr. Sparkman: Of course that would be a matter of estimate at any time. It was estimated before our subcommittee that there were 162 cases of dire need at that time.

"Mr. Thomas: How have those cases been taken care of up to now?

"Mr. Sparkman: Those cases have been taken care of by the church organizations and the groups that have been supporting the conscientious objectors.

"Mr. Thomas: Are most of those cases for one church or are they divided up among different churches?

"Mr. Sparkman: No, they are scattered among a great number of churches. As a matter of fact I have an article here which I propose to ask permission to insert in the *Record* which shows the various churches and various organizations from which these conscientious objectors come. I also propose to place in the *Record* or to ask permission to place in the *Record* a showing as to what type of projects these conscientious objectors are working on and how they are scattered throughout these various services that they are performing.

"Mr. Thomas: So the cost to any one church would be very small then. It would not be large?

"Mr. Sparkman: That might be true as to the support of these 162 cases. The estimate is—it would take, I would say, between $120,000 and $150,000 a year to take care of these cases. But let us remember that these various organizations, in addition to taking care of these needy dependent cases, are also taking care of the conscientious objectors themselves and are running the camps without cost to the Government. It is estimated that had the Government been called upon to run the camps which the conscientious objectors themselves are running, the cost would have been $4,000,000.

"Mr. Thomas: Does the gentleman see any good reason why we should give any consideration to conscientious objectors anyway?

"Mr. Sparkman: This bill does not purport to give consideration to conscientious objectors, but to the wives and children of conscientious objectors who are left in a needy condition, many of whom may not even agree with the views of the conscientious objectors.

"I may say to the gentleman that I certainly cannot share the belief of any conscientious objector, but it has been the traditional and historic policy of our country that in war the right of conscience is acknowledged. When the gentleman's own committee passed the Selective Training and Service Act of 1940, a provision was written in it to take care of these conscientious objectors.

"Mr. Thomas: Under this bill, the family and dependents of a conscientious objector get the same aid as the needy family of soldiers; is that not correct?

"Mr. Sparkman: That is not true.

"Mr. Thomas: According to the bill it is.

"Mr. Sparkman: No, the maximum limitation is the amount the Government would have contributed to the soldier's dependent.

"Mr. Thomas: So it would be the same.

"Mr. Sparkman: It could be the same as that which the Government donates?

"Mr. Thomas: Mr. Speaker, I object.

"Mr. Sparkman: Will the gentleman withhold his objection to permit me to finish that statement?

"Mr. Thomas: Mr. Speaker, I withhold my objection to permit the gentleman to finish his statement.·

"Mr. Sparkman: I should like to call the gentlemen's attention to the fact that this does not appropriate any money out of the Treasury, but that this is money which has been earned by the conscientious objectors themselves.

"Mr. Thomas: Nevertheless, conscientious objectors should not be given any consideration. That is the way I feel.

"Mr. Sparkman: This money has been placed in a special deposit in the Treasury of the United States under an agreement that it is not to be spent for war purposes.

"Mr. Brooks (La.): Mr. Speaker, will the gentleman yield?

"Mr. Sparkman: I yield.

"Mr. Brooks: I may say that I sat on the sub-committee when the bill was drafted. It was rewritten and changed from the way in which it was introduced by the distinguished gentleman from New York (Mr. Cole). This bill, in my judgment, places the families of conscientious objectors on the same basis as the families of servicemen. It gives the conscientious objectors' families the same allowance the Government contributes to the family of a serviceman. While we want to take care of charity, as charity should be cared for, I doubt if this Congress wants to take care of the families of conscientious objectors on the same basis as families of soldiers.

"Mr. Sparkman: Mr. Speaker, I regret that objection has been made. I believe that one familiar with the facts would agree to the objective sought by this measure.

"This bill is an attempt to correct a situation among conscientious objectors who have been drafted. I realize these men constitute an unpopular minority, but I sincerely hope we will not allow the general disfavor with which this group is regarded to blind us to inequities in our treatment of them.

"I do not propose here to debate the issue of the conscientious objector. That was done at the time the Selective Service Act was passed and Congress, in its wisdom, accorded to sincere, religious objectors a legal alternative to military service by providing for them 'work of national importance under civilian direction.'

"During the three years since conscientious objector camps were first set up to do 'work of national importance' under the supervision of the Selective Service System, the total camp population has remained small. To date, less than 7,000 men are in Civilian Public Service, the alternative service program, and they have all been judged both sincere and religious by their local draft boards, after investigation by the F. B. I. as provided by law.

"For three years these men have worked in forestry and soil conservation camps, fighting forest fires and soil erosion and engaged in similar projects. Increasing numbers of them are volunteering to do dirty jobs in State mental hospitals and other public institutions, some of which have been almost crippled by shortages of orderlies and attendants.

"I think you will find that in almost every case these men have done a good, honest and conscientious job. Yet for three years they have been working without any pay whatsoever, without accident compensation, without any of the minor benefits extended to servicemen. Congress has never, in fact, appropriated money for the maintenance of the great majority of these men. Their food and clothing bills are assumed either by themselves or by sponsoring church groups. It might surprise Congress to know that we give fewer benefits to the conscientious objectors than we do to interned aliens, to Japanese-Americans, and to prisoners of war.

"The particular discrepancy at which this bill is directed, however, is the fact that conscientious objectors do not receive any dependency benefits, despite the fact that they have exactly the same percentage of wives and children as men sent to the military service—about 35 per cent. This means, in effect, that we are penalizing wives and children because we do not agree with their husbands and fathers. Let us apply the restrictions directly to the men, if we will, but we should not extend the punishment to their families.

"Our committee's recommendation, we feel, is a happy solution. We propose to devote to the dependency needs of these men the money which they themselves earn, but are not allowed to keep. The proposal was suggested by the National Service Board for Religious Objectors, and has been approved by Selective Service, the War Department, and the Bureau of the Budget.

"About 700 conscientious objectors are assigned to farm work, and others have been called from the camps at various times to help in planting and harvesting emergencies. In each case, the farmer pays the individual objector the prevailing wage, but he is not allowed to keep the money beyond his actual expenses in doing the work. The remainder is sent to the United States Treasury for a special account, which by the end of April amounted to $370,731.19. The bill provides that the disbursing of this fund be made on a strict basis of need, rather than by the Army system of flat dependency grants, and that each request for aid be carefully investigated and supervised by Selective Service.

"The bill takes the form of an amendment to H. R. 3199, introduced last fall by the gentleman from New York, Representative Cole, to apply these same conscientious objector earnings to the Office of Foreign Relief and Rehabilitation Administration, now U. N. R. R. A. This was in response to the request of the men themselves who, if they could not keep the money themselves, were anxious that it be used for relief purposes. It goes without saying, however, that they would prefer their money to be spent for their own needy wives and children.

"So far, these requests for financial aid for dependents have been shouldered by the religious groups most concerned—the Mennonites, Church of the Brethren, Society of Friends—Quakers—and the Fellowship of Reconciliation. These groups are already saddled with the maintenance of the majority of conscientious objectors—expenses which run about a million and half dollars a year—and the additional $136,000 which is needed to tide over only the worst of their dependency cases is a heavy load for such religious bodies. So far these church groups have spent over $4,000,000 to finance this program.

"Some of the worst dependency situations are found in the camps financed entirely by the Government, but even here the church groups have assumed responsibility and are aiding needy wives and dependents because the Government has made no provision for them.

"Their only recourse is to look to Congress to help—help which this bill would supply. We are simply proposing that the money which these men themselves earn be made available for their own pressing dependency needs."

Meanwhile, the most pressing needs of the dependents of conscientious objectors are being cared for by private charity, as well as by public relief. The National Service Board for Religious Objectors has set up a dependency council whose budget for the month of July, 1944, calls for $1,560 for the dependents of forty-five men in Civilian Public Service camps and in prison.

Since Congressional action is probably unobtainable, the only solution to this problem would be the assign-

ment of conscientious objectors to jobs and permission
to retain the wages earned. This is the system followed
in Great Britain which has resulted in fair treatment
of conscientious objectors and no expense whatever to
the government for supervising their work. The conditions of work in each case are left up to the individual local tribunal and in most cases the conscientious
objector is allowed to take a job near his home and
frequently in a line of work for which he is especially
adapted. This solution is so practical and sensible, as
well as inexpensive, that one wonders if our public
officials correctly interpret public opinion when they
refuse to follow the excellent example which the British
have placed before us.

Chapter 9

Citizenship and Public Office

FOR MANY YEARS it has been impossible for a conscientious objector to become a citizen of the United States by naturalization, since the immigration officials have interpreted the oath of naturalization, which requires a promise to "support and defend the Constitution," as requiring an unqualified willingness to bear arms, and the Supreme Court of the United States has upheld them in this interpretation.* But this rule, although well established, is perhaps no longer valid, in view of the policy of Congress to respect the scruples of conscience in regard to military service as expressed in the Selective Training and Service Act of 1940.

In January, 1944, two conscientious objectors were admitted to citizenship in the Federal Court at Seattle, Washington, thereby breaking the precedent under which pacifists have long been excluded from citizenship.† Both men were British subjects, and both were serving in noncombatant capacities in the medical corps of the United States Army as conscientious objectors, under the classification I-A-O. When examined by the Immigration Service, the men testified that they could not subscribe to the oath of allegiance if it were interpreted as requiring a willingness to bear arms, since

---

* *U. S.* v. *Schwimmer,* 279 United States Reports 644; *U. S.* v. *Macintosh,* 283 United States Reports 605.

† *In re Kinloch,* 53 Federal Supplement 521.

50

this would conflict with their religious beliefs. When the matter came before the court, the Immigration Service contended that these men were not entitled to citizenship, relying upon the Supreme Court cases. The court held that these cases were inapplicable because Congress had subsequently established a different rule for naturalization when it provided that members of the armed forces may become naturalized without the necessity of filing a declaration of intention or residing for a time in the United States.* It is clear that this permits conscientious objectors serving in the armed forces to be naturalized, since the law specifically excludes from its benefits "any conscientious objector who performed no military duty whatever or refused to wear the uniform."† Accordingly, the court decided that the two men in question could be admitted to citizenship despite the rule which prevents pacifists generally from becoming citizens.

This case is not to be taken as a departure from the rule which excludes pacifists from naturalization; that rule still stands except as modified by Congress, and Congress has modified it only to the extent of permitting conscientious objectors serving in the armed forces to become citizens. But this is an opening wedge, and it is to be hoped that either Congress or the courts will eventually do away with a rule which is both illogical and intolerant. If pacifists are to be allowed to serve the country in war-time in such ways as their consciences

---

* Title 8 United States Code, Secs. 1001-1005, enacted March 27, 1942.
† Ibid, sec. 1004.

permit, and thereby discharge the duties of citizenship, then they should also be allowed to attain citizenship otherwise than by the accident of birth.

Clyde W. Summers, although otherwise qualified, was denied the right to practice law in Illinois solely because he is a conscientious objector. After having been rejected on this ground by the Committee appointed to examine into the character and fitness of applicants, Summers took the matter to the Supreme Court of Illinois, which denied his petition for admission to the bar. There was no hearing granted by the court and no opinion was written. Summers thereupon filed a petition for a writ of certiorari in the Supreme Court of the United States, asking that court to review the action of the Illinois court. In the brief which I filed as his attorney in support of Summers' petition the case is argued thus:

"Although the question has never been decided by this Court whether the right to practice law is a right of liberty and property which may not be denied without due process of law nor denied the equal protection of the laws, several such cases were decided by this Court before the adoption of the Fourteenth Amendment, and shortly after its adoption but under another clause, namely the privileges and immunities clause. Such cases include: *In re Secombe,* 19 How 9, where mandamus was denied to review the disbarment of an attorney because it was held not to be the proper remedy; *In re Garland,* 4 Wall. 333, which held unconstitutional an Act of Congress restricting membership in the Federal bar to those who took an oath that they had never given aid or comfort to the Confederacy on the ground that such a law was *ex post facto* and a bill of attainder; and *Bradwell* v. *Illinois*, 16 Wall. 130, where a woman was denied admission to the bar of Illinois by the State Supreme Court on the ground of her sex, and this Court held that the privilege of the practice of law was not a privilege of United States citizens protected by the privileges and immunities clause of the Fourteenth amendment.

"These are the precedents, and all of them were decided on different grounds than those urged here. This question is therefore a novel one for this Court and we must turn for guidance to analogous cases, such as those involving licenses to engage in occupations other than the practice of law.

"It is true that a State may require a license or the fulfillment of certain qualifications or the passing of prescribed tests as conditions precedent to the carrying on of an occupation, business or profession. Furthermore, moral character and fitness may form the basis for admission to the right to exercise an occupation or profession. *Hawker* v. *N. Y.*, 170 U. S. 189 (practice of medicine); *Douglas* v. *Noble*, 261 U. S. 165 (practice of dentistry). Nevertheless, the issuance of such a license and the admission to the privileges of such occupation, business or profession must be based upon reasonable conditions and may not be arbitrarily denied under the Fourteenth Amendment.

"The petitioner set forth his views in detail in the hearing before the Committee on Character and Fitness, in which he disclosed that he is unwilling to participate in war because of his religious and conscientious views, and that his local draft board had recognized the genuineness of his scruples by classifying him in Class IV-E as a conscientious objector. In making this determination the local draft board necessarily found that the petitioner's opposition to war is based upon 'religious training and belief.' The statute itself so requires. (Section 5g of the Selective Training and Service Act of 1940.)

"Thus the petitioner's opposition to war, for which the State of Illinois has rejected him as morally unfit to practice law, is based not upon personal whim or expediency, nor upon political or social views, but upon the deep and abiding compulsion of his inner religious convictions, since the demonstration of such a religious basis for conscientious objection is required in order to merit exemption. *U. S.* v. *Kauten,* 133 Fed. 2nd 703, 708. *U. S. ex. rel. Phillips* v. *Downer,* 135 Fed. 2nd 521; *U. S. ex rel. Reel* v. *Badt,* 141 Fed. 2nd 845.

"The petitioner is therefore recognized as coming within the class of persons commonly called conscientious objectors, to whom Congress has seen fit to extend protection for their religious scruples, and there can be no question that a denial to the petitioner of rights to which he is otherwise entitled, solely because he is a conscientious objector, sharply interferes with his religious liberty.

"It is no longer open to question that freedom of religion guaranteed under the First Amendment is protected against State encroachment by the Fourteenth Amendment. *Barnette* v. *West Virginia,* 319 U. S. 624.

"The infringement upon petitioner's liberties here involved is arbitrary, discriminatory and unreasonable, having no justification either in morals or reason, and therefore falls within the intendment of the Fourteenth Amendment prohibiting the denial of religious liberty without due process of law.

"Not only is petitioner deprived of his liberty by the action here complained of, but he is also deprived of a valuable right of property, namely, the right to engage in the practice of the law.

"It has been held many times by this Court that the right to engage in such professions as the practice of medicine or dentistry, as well as other occupations and businesses, constitutes a right of property which may not be taken without due process of law under the Fourteenth Amendment.

"There can be hardly any question that property rights have been damaged, if not totally destroyed, when the petitioner has been prevented from entering upon the practice of a profession for which he has spent years of his time and much of his capital in preparation, and this deprivation of petitioner's property was made without the due process of law required by the Fourteenth Amendment, since based upon an arbitrary, discriminatory and unreasonable act which springs only from intolerance and has no foundation in reason or justice.

"The equal protection of the laws requires that the laws of the State of Illinois governing admission to the practice of law be applied with equal hand to all qualified candidates for admission to the bar. It is unthinkable to our law that such great privileges as the right to practice the profession of law should be granted to some and withheld from others, equally fitted for that profession, solely on the basis of race, creed, color, religion or persuasion of belief. Indeed it is almost unthinkable that such a case as this could arise, except from the hysteria of war time, and even then no calm and judicial mind can fail to rise in outcry against the unfairness and intolerance of the discrimination here practiced against the petitioner by the State of Illinois.

"While it is well understood that admission to the practice of law may be restricted to those who possess the necessary moral qualifications and good character, the test of moral fitness and character to be imposed must bear a reasonable relation to the ends sought to be attained, namely the preservation of high standards of ethics and integrity in the legal profession. There is no doubt, for instance, that exclusion from the bar on the basis of race would be a denial of equal protection of the laws under the Fourteenth Amendment, because the racial test would have no reasonable relation to the securing of proper standards for the legal profession. See *Yick Wo* v. *Hopkins*, 118 U. S. 356, where a license to operate a laundry was denied to an applicant solely because he was Chinese, and *U. S. v. Hirabayashi,* 320 U. S. 81 (at page 100) involving the current racial discrimination against persons of Japanese ancestry on the West Coast.

"Even more deeply ingrained in our constitution than protection against racial discrimination is the protection which that instrument affords against religious discrimination. If, therefore, one may not be excluded from an occupation or profession by reason of his race, certainly he may not be excluded by reason of his religious beliefs. That a man entertains unusual and unpopular religious beliefs is no ground for excluding him from the practice of law, since this bears no reasonable relation to his fitness to become a lawyer. On the contrary, the exemplary character in general of members of the Religious Society of Friends (Quakers) and other pacifist groups, is well recognized and has long been respected by public opinion and by the courts. See the dissenting opinion of Chief Justice Hughes in *U. S. v. Macintosh,* 283 U. S. 605, 630-632, and the history of the Quaker colony of Pennsylvania.

"In other states than Illinois, conscientious objectors have been freely admitted to the bar, and in New York their admission has even been expedited when they were about to be drafted. In general pacifists have frequently been given positions of public trust, and include many eminent statesmen, judges and lawyers."

Also worthy of notice is the case of Edward O. Schweitzer, who was discharged from his position as a teacher in the Miami, Florida, schools by the County Board of Public Instruction solely on the ground that he is a conscientious objector, although he had never given public expression to those views or attempted to instill them in his pupils.

The Miami *Daily News* came to Schweitzer's aid and devoted many columns to his support, thereby giving much publicity to the case. Nevertheless, Schweitzer was ousted by the school board, and appealed to the courts. The trial court ordered the school board to reinstate Schweitzer, but this ruling was reversed on appeal, and the matter is now before the Supreme Court of Florida. A thorough analysis of the issues will be found in the columns of the Miami *Daily News* from August 10 to September 2, 1943.

Chapter 10

The C.O. in Canada

ALTHOUGH THE TREATMENT of conscientious objectors in Canada, was, for a time, more like ours than like the British, the Canadians have almost abandoned the concentration camp idea and most of their conscientious objectors are now assigned individually to worth-while jobs at prevailing wages, which go to support them and their dependents as well as to the Red Cross. The keeping of men in the camps is described by the Canadians as an "emotional luxury" which they cannot afford because of the labor shortage.

The status of Canadian C.O's. was recently investigated by Paul Comly French, Executive Secretary of the National Service Board for Religious Objectors, whose report on the subject was summarized in the August 15, 1944, issue of *The Reporter*, newssheet issued by the Board:

"More than 9,000 men have been 'postponed' as conscientious objectors to date, by far the greatest part of whom have been assigned to Alternate Service Work Camps or given alternate service contracts for individual assignments.

"Of the total, Mennonites comprise about 63 per cent., Doukhobors 20 per cent., and the remainder 17 per cent. Neither the Brethren or Friends have any sizeable group in Canada.

"The Canadian system has no classification comparable to our I-A-O, noncombatant service in the armed forces, although men who are given a postponed C.O. status are asked if they would accept service in the medical or dental corps. So far about 200 men have accepted this service. Several religious leaders declared that considerable pressure is often used to force men into the medical corps, but this government officials denied.

"Similarly, only a comparatively small number of men are in prison for conscientious reasons. Men who refuse to obey the instructions of the Alternate Service Officer are usually sentenced to one of the camps where C.O's. are normally sent.

"If a man walks out of camp, he is usually sentenced to jail for terms ranging from 30 days to six months, usually with the proviso that he be sent back to camp at the end of the sentence. In one case 'an extremely severe' sentence of one year was imposed. There is no parole available.

"Men whose C.O. claims are denied and who still refuse to report to the army are escorted to a military barracks by the Royal Canadian Mounted Police. There they are often given one, two or three 14-day court martial sentences if their refusal persists, then in a majority of such cases, military authorities recommend they be given a C.O. postponement and sent to camp. About 300 men have been involved in this group in the five years that Canada has been at war.

"Regarding the camps themselves, these are apparently in a constant state of flux. In the early days, postponed C.O's. were not directed to perform any type of service at all, but public sentiment forced the government to assign them to camps. In the past year, however, need for the men elsewhere has resulted in individual assignments to farms and other work and only five camps remain with a total population of about 300.

"Camps were set up largely in western Canada and engaged in forestry work, road-building, etc. The five remaining now operate somewhat in the nature of detention centers for those sentenced to camp. In camp men are paid at the rate of 50 cents a day.

"Bulk of the men are now serving under alternate service contracts with most of the men on farms. Here they are allowed to keep $25 a month out of the prevailing wages paid them, with extras for dependents, overtime, insurance, etc. The balance is turned over to the Canadian Red Cross, which so far has received between $300,000 and $400,000 from this source.

"No one is officially discharged from alternate service. Psychiatric cases are simply transferred to institutions, while medical cases are given less strenuous assignments. Once an assignee reaches 38, however, the end of the Canadian conscription system, he is freed from further responsibility to the Alternate Service Officer."

Perhaps the most significant thing about the Canadian experience is that there has been almost no public criticism of the policy of allowing conscientious objectors to work individually at paying jobs. There has not been a story about C.O's. in the Ottawa newspapers for two and a half years, Paul French was told by a government official. The Canadian experience therefore impairs the validity of the reason given by American officials for not treating C.O's. better, that public opinion would not permit it. Perhaps our Selective Service officials pay too much attention to the crank and the fanatical patriot, but would find that the bulk of the people, here as in Canada, would not disapprove a program for conscientious objectors designed for usefulness rather than for punishment.*

---

* A study of public opinion made by a Princeton professor supports this view; see page 17.

Chapter 11

Judicial Review of Draft Boards

JUDICIAL REVIEW, although highly desirable, has been generally denied to conscientious objectors by the courts. Under recent decisions of the Supreme Court of the United States this situation has completely changed. Here, again, a notable victory has been won through the courts, as in the case of liberalizing the interpretation of the phrase "religious training and belief."

In the case of *Falbo* v. *United States* (320 United States Reports 549, decided January 3, 1944), the court held that a Jehovah's Witness who refused to report to a camp for conscientious objectors could not question the validity of his classification (he claimed exemption as a minister) for the reason that he had not completed the Selective Service process, which comes to an end only when one has reported for induction or assignment to a Civilian Public Service camp. On the same day the court refused to hear argument on a similar case of a conscientious objector who had refused to be inducted into the army.*

Justice Murphy filed a strong dissenting opinion which is worth quoting in full (320 United States Reports, at pp. 555 to 561):

"This case presents another aspect of the perplexing problem of reconciling basic principles of justice with

---

* *Zernit* v. *United States*, 320 United States Reports, 801.

military needs in wartime. Individual rights have been recognized by our jurisprudence only after long and costly struggles. They should not be struck down by anything less than the gravest necessity. We assent to their temporary suspension only to the extent that they constitute a clear and present danger to the effective prosecution of the war and only as a means of preserving those rights undiminished for ourselves and future generations. Before giving such an assent, therefore, we should be convinced of the existence of a reasonable necessity and be satisfied that the suspension is in accordance with the legislative intention.

"The immediate issue is whether the Selective Training and Service Act of 1940 must be interpreted so as to deprive alleged violators of the right to a full hearing and of the right to present every reasonable defense. Petitioner, a member of Jehovah's Witnesses, claimed to be a minister exempt from both military training and civilian work under the Act. After exhausting all the administrative remedies and appeals afforded by the Act, he was classified as a conscientious objector (Class IV-E), rather than as a minister (Class IV-D). Petitioner alleges that this classification was contrary to law and was the result of arbitrary action by his local board. On the assumption that these allegations are true, the subsequent order to report for assignment to work of national importance, which he disobeyed, must therefore be considered invalid. Our problem is simply whether petitioner can introduce evidence to that effect as a defense to a criminal prosecution for failure to obey the order.

"Common sense and justice dictate that a citizen accused of a crime should have the fullest hearing possible, plus the opportunity to present every reasonable defense. Only an unenlightened jurisprudence condemns an individual without according him those rights. Such a denial is especially oppressive where a full hearing might disclose that the administrative action underlying the prosecution is the product of excess wartime emotions. Experience demonstrates that in time of war individual liberties cannot always be entrusted safely to uncontrolled administrative discretion. Illustrative of this proposition is the remark attributed to one of the members of petitioner's local board to the effect that 'I do not have any damned use for Jehovah's Witnesses.' The presumption against foreclosing the defense of illegal and arbitrary administrative action is therefore strong. Only the clearest statutory language or an unmistakable threat to the public safety can justify a court in shutting the door to such a defense. Because I am convinced that neither the Selective Training and Service Act of 1940 nor the war effort compels the result reached by the majority of this Court, I am forced to dissent.

"It is evident that there is no explicit provision in the Act permitting the raising of this particular defense and that the legislative history is silent on the matter. Suffice it to say, however, that nothing in the statute or in its legislative record proscribes this defense or warrants the conviction of petitioner without benefit of a full hearing. Judicial protection of an individual against arbitrary and illegal administrative action does not depend upon the presence or absence of express statutory authorization. The power to administer complete justice and to consider all reasonable pleas and defenses must be presumed in the absence of legislation to the contrary.

"Moreover, the structure of the Act is entirely consistent with judicial review of induction orders in criminal proceedings. As the majority states, the Act is designed 'to operate as one continuous process for the selection of men for national service,' and it is desirable that this process be free from 'litigious interruption.' But we are faced here with a complete and permanent interruption springing not from any affirmative judicial intervention, but from a failure to obey an order. A criminal proceeding before a court is therefore inevitable and the only problem is the availability of a particular defense in that proceeding. Hence judicial review at this stage has none of the elements of a 'litigious interruption' of the administrative process.

"No other barriers to judicial review of the induction order in a criminal proceeding are revealed by the structure of the Act. The 'continuous process' of selection is unique, unlike any ordinary administrative proceeding. Normal concepts of administrative law are foreign to this setting. Thus rules preventing judicial review of interlocutory administrative orders and requiring exhaustion of the administrative process have no application here. Those rules are based upon the unnecessary inconvenience which the administrative agency would suffer if its proceedings were interrupted by premature judicial intervention. But since the administrative process has already come to a final ending the reason for applying such rules no longer exists. And even if the order in this case were considered interlocutory rather than final, which is highly questionable, judicial review at this point is no less necessary. Criminal punishment for disobedience of an arbitrary and invalid order is objectionable regardless of whether the order be interlocutory or final.

"Nor do familiar doctrines of the exclusiveness of statutory remedies have any relevance here. Had Congress created a statutory judicial review procedure prior to or following induction, the failure to take advantage of such a review or the judicial approval of the induction order upon appeal might bar a collateral attack on the order in a criminal proceeding. But Congress has erected no such system of judicial review. Courts are left to their own devices in fashioning whatever review they deem just and necessary.

"Thus there is no express or implied barrier to the raising of this defense or to the granting of a full judicial review of induction orders in criminal proceedings. Courts have not hesitated to make such review available in

habeas corpus proceedings following induction despite
the absence of express statutory authorization. Where,
as here, induction will never occur and the habeas corpus
procedure is unavailable, judicial review in a criminal
proceeding becomes imperative if petitioner is to be given
any protection against arbitrary and invalid administrative action.

"It is significant that in analgous situations in the past,
although without passing upon the precise issue, we have
supplied such a necessary review in criminal proceedings.
Cf. *Union Bridge Co.* v. *United States,* 204 U. S. 364;
Monongahela Bridge Co. v. *United States,* 216 U. S. 177;
McAllister, 'Statutory Roads to Review of Federal Administrative Orders,' 28 California L. Rev. 129, 165, 166.
See also *Fire Department of City of New York* v. *Gilmour,*
149 N. Y. 453, 44 N.E. 177; *People* v. *McCoy,* 125 Ill. 289,
17 N.E. 786.

"Finally, the effective prosecution of the war in no way
demands that petitioner be denied a full hearing in this
case. We are concerned with a speedy and effective mobilization of armed forces. But that mobilization is neither
impeded nor augmented by the availability of judicial
review of local board orders in criminal proceedings. In
the rare case where the accused person can prove the
arbitrary and illegal nature of the administrative action,
the induction order should never have been issued and the
armed forces are deprived of no one who should have
been inducted. And where the defendant is unable to
prove such a defense or where, pursuant to this Court's
opinion, he is forbidden even to assert this defense, the
prison rather than the Army or Navy is the recipient of
his presence. Thus the military strength of this nation
gains naught by the denial of judicial review in this
instance.

"To say that the availability of such a review would
encourage disobedience of induction orders, or that denial
of a review would have a deterrent effect, is neither

demonstrable nor realistic. There is no evidence that petitioner failed to obey the local board order because of a belief that he could secure a judicial reversal of the order and thus escape the duty to defend his country. Those who seek such a review are invariably those whose conscientious or religious scruples would prevent them from reporting for induction regardless of the availability of this defense. And I am not aware that disobedience has multiplied in the Fourth Circuit, where this defense has been allowed. *Baxley* v. *United States,* 134 F. 2nd 998; *Goff* v. *United States,* 135 F. 2nd 610. Moreover, English courts under identical circumstances during the last war unhesitatingly provided a full hearing and reviewed orders to report for permanent service. *Offord* v. *Hiscock,* 86 L. J. K. B. 941; *Hawkes* v. *Moxey,* 86 L. J. K. B. 1530. Yet that did not noticeably impede the efficiency or speed of England's mustering of an adequate military force.

"That an individual should languish in prison for five years without being accorded the opportunity of proving that the prosecution was based upon arbitrary and illegal administrative action is not in keeping with the high standards of our judicial system. Especially is this so where neither public necessity nor rule of law or statute leads inexorably to such a harsh result. The law knows no finer hour than when it cuts through formal concepts and transitory emotions to protect unpopular citizens against discrimination and persecution. I can perceive no other course for the law to take in this case."

The majority were not persuaded by this argument and their decision in this case was a most harsh one, as it prevented a conscientious objector from obtaining judicial review* unless he is willing to submit himself

---

* It should be remarked, however, that the *Falbo* decision does not extend to the case of a denial of procedural or constitutional rights, but merely covers the case of error in classification. It is probable that

to the army, where he would face ignominy and contempt by military men and court martial, which may result in unlimited imprisonment or even a sentence of death.†

Perhaps the court did not realize when it decided this case the full effect of its ruling. However this may be, the court apparently felt compelled to modify the *Falbo* ruling, and took occasion to do so on March 27, 1944, when it decided the case of *Billings v. Truesdell,*‡ in which it was held that a conscientious objector who had appeared at the place of induction following classification in I-A and was unwillingly inducted, despite his refusal to take the oath of induction, should be released from the army upon writ of habeas corpus, on the ground that he had been illegally inducted. The court's opinion, written by Mr. Justice Douglas, construed the provision in Section 11 of the Selective Training and Service Act that military jurisdiction does not apply until a person has been "actually inducted" and that prior to that time violations are cognizable only by the civil courts. The court found that Billings had not been "actually inducted," reasoning that a draftee is not inducted upon mere acceptance by the armed forces, but only after he has taken the oath.

---

in spite of this decision, judicial review may be obtained without reporting for induction if the draft boards have failed to grant the benefits of a fair hearing or appeal, or have otherwise failed to follow the proper procedure, *(Chih Chung Tung v. U. S.,* 142 Fed. Rep., 2nd Series, 919), or if constitutional questions are involved which would render the entire statute invalid *(Heflin v. Sanford,* 142 Fed. Rep., 2nd Series, 798). Cf. *Giese v. United States,* 143 Fed. Rep., 2nd Series, 633. This has become unimportant except as to cases already arisen, as judicial review even of improper classification is now possible.

† Article 64 of the Articles of War (10 U. S. Code, Sec. 1536).

‡ 321 United States Reports, 542.

The government had contended that Billings was inducted when the oath was read to him, although he did not voluntarily take the oath. After pointing out that the regulations require one to submit to induction, the court concluded that induction implies voluntary acceptance of military status by undergoing "whatever ceremony or requirements of admission the War Department has prescribed." The court said that Congress intended that those who refuse induction should be tried in the civil courts only and pointed out that forcible induction would thwart the intention of Congress.

Mr. Justice Roberts dissented, stating simply that the judgment should be affirmed for the reasons given in the lower court's opinion, while Mr. Justice Frankfurter concurred in a separate opinion.

The court's reasoning in the *Billings* case appears somewhat strained in its distinction between acceptance by the armed forces and induction, a distinction of terminology rather than actual fact. While the court's reasoning is artificial and the result reached was unexpected, the probable explanation for the *Billings* decision appears from the following paragraph of the opinion:

"Moreover, it should be remembered that he who reports at the induction station is following the procedure outlined in the *Falbo* case for the exhaustion of his administrative remedies. Unless he follows that procedure he may not challenge the legality of his classification in the courts. But we can hardly say that he must report to the military in order to exhaust his administrative remedies and then say that if he does so report he may be forcibly inducted against his will. That would indeed make a trap of the *Falbo* case by subjecting those who reported for completion of the Selective Service process to more severe penalties than those who stayed away in defiance of the Board's order to report."

Apparently the court realized that the *Falbo* decision, if carried out to its logical extremes, would require a registrant who desires to obtain judicial review to submit to induction against his will and risk being subjected to military law, and that all this would be required of him in order to exhaust his administrative remedies. The court has indicated in the *Billings* case that it had not intended by the *Falbo* decision to go this far. It may well be that the court recognized the injustice of the *Falbo* ruling, which it has now mollified by holding that the administrative process comes to an end with acceptance by the armed forces, which occurs before induction. When so qualified, the *Falbo* case loses its severity, since the requirements for judicial review of draft board errors may now be complied with by reporting at an induction center for acceptance by the armed forces, although thereafter the oath of induction is refused. When this happens, under the *Billings* case, the military authorities cannot forcibly induct and the civil authorities will retain jurisdiction.

From the foregoing it is clear that a conscientious objector who is denied exemption may fulfill the requirements of the Supreme Court for obtaining judicial review by obeying the draft board's order to report for induction, although he refuses to take the oath of induction. He will then doubtless be prosecuted for refusal to take the oath and this being an offense which is pun-

ishable only by the civil authorities, he will be prosecuted in the Federal courts, whereupon he may present
the defense that he has been illegally classified if it
appears that his classification was arbitrary and unreasonable. Prior to the *Billings* case, this procedure would
not have been possible, since the practice of the armed
forces was to induct those who appeared at the induction
station but refused to take the oath. Now, however, the
Supreme Court has held that induction under such circumstances is illegal. Unless the Selective Service regulations or the Articles of War are modified to dispense
with the oath as a necessary part of the induction ceremony, it will therefore be possible for conscientious
objectors to obtain judicial review prior to induction.

The effect of the *Falbo* decision has now been destroyed and judicial review without submitting to induction has, for the first time, become possible for conscientious objectors.

It need hardly be pointed out that if the above
analysis is correct, the *Billings* case takes on great importance for conscientious objectors, who may now without subjecting themselves to military rule obtain redress from the courts in cases where draft boards have
committed errors.

Several score men who refused the oath of induction
and had been court martialed and incarcerated in military prisons are now entitled to release under the *Billings* decision, although they will face prosecution in the
civil courts for refusing to accept military service, and
further imprisonment unless they have a defense. The
army has refused to release such men without court

orders, which, however, they have readily obtained by way of writs of habeas corpus, mostly unopposed by the United States Attorneys.

Chapter 12

Classification Procedure

In order to facilitate the classification procedure, two changes in the regulations have been made which affect conscientious objectors.

It has been provided that when an appeal is filed which involves the question of conscientious objection, the appeal board may grant a conscientious objector classification (IV-E or I-A-O) without the necessity of first forwarding the file to the Department of Justice for investigation and hearing as previously required. It is still necessary for an investigation and hearing to take place if the appeal board does not determine forthwith to grant the desired classification as a conscientious objector.

The other change is of much greater importance. Under the original procedure, a conscientious objector who failed to gain exemption was ordered to report for induction. Since if he did report and passed the physical examination, he would be immediately and unwillingly inducted into the armed forces, he had no choice if he desired to avoid the risk of induction but to refrain from obeying the order to report and to surrender himself to the civil authorities for prosecution. When he was prosecuted, therefore, he had not had the benefit of a physical examination other than the "screening" test by a local draft board physician, which was very perfunctory and designed only to eliminate the most obviously unfit. Under this procedure many conscientious objectors have been imprisoned who would have been rejected for physical defects, if they had been granted a physical examination.

On January 10, 1944, there became effective amendments to the Selective Service regulations setting up an entirely new system of physical examination and induction. The new procedure is set out in two new chapters of the regulations, *Part 633—Delivery and Induction* and *Part 629—Physical Examination*.

Under the new regulations every registrant before he is ordered to report for induction is given a pre-induction physical examination. As to men classified I-A and I-A-O, the local board will send them in groups to the induction center for the pre-induction physical examination in response to calls from headquarters for a specified number of men after selecting (1) volunteers, (2) nonfathers, and (3) fathers—in that order and, within each group, making the selection according to order number.* Since there are no calls issued for class IV-E, these men will be sent to the induction center for physical examination when their order numbers are reached, also subject to the same requirements as to postponment of fathers.

If the examination is passed, the papers will be marked to show whether the registrant has been accepted for general service in the army, limited service in the army, naval service, or work of national importance as a conscientious objector, and will then be returned to the local board.† If the examination is not

---

* Selective Service Regulations, ¶629.2 (b).
† Selective Service Regulations, ¶629.31.

passed, the papers will likewise be returned to the local board, which will re-open the classification and reclassify the registrant in class IV-F.

Appeals from I-A, I-A-O, or IV-E classification are taken as heretofore within ten days of notice of classification. But the appeal is not considered until *after* the physical examination at the induction center has been completed and passed.

The regulations prescribe a new procedure for induction as well as for physical examination. Induction is now accomplished in most cases at the basic training camp and not at the induction center as heretofore. An entire new chapter of the regulations, entitled *"Part 633—Delivery and Induction,"* supersedes the former Part 633.

Under the revised procedure conscientious objectors may receive the benefit of a physical examination and possible IV-F classification without risking induction into the armed forces. If the local draft board denies exemption, the registrant may file an appeal, but before the appeal is considered, he will receive a pre-induction physical examination. If he fails the examination he will be classified IV-F by the local board, but if he passes the examination his file will then be forwarded by the local board to the appeal board, which will then determine whether or not to classify him as a conscientious objector, and if it does not grant such classification will forward the file to the Department of Justice for investigation and hearing. From this point the procedure will be as heretofore.

Chapter 13

Presidential Appeals

DESPITE THE OBVIOUS illegality* of such procedure, Presidential appeals have continued to be handled by military officers, not, however, without attacks upon this procedure both through pressure for administrative reforms and appeals to the courts.

The case of Arthur Brandon† was decided on another ground by the Circuit Court of Appeals, which held on the question whether the decision of military officers was improper that this was moot because Congress had, before the appeal was argued, amended the statute to legalize the handling of Presidential appeals by military men. On this phase of the case the court's opinion written by Judge Frank, states:

"Appellant argues that the appeal taken by the State Director to the President was not properly considered because the decision was made by General Hershey, the Director of Selective Service, who was a military officer. In this connection appellant points to a provision of Sec. 10 (a) (2) of the statute that the President 'shall establish within the Selective Service System civilian local boards and such other civilian agencies, including appeal boards and agencies of appeal, as may be necessary. * * * Appeal boards and agencies of appeal within the Selective Service System shall be composed of civilians * * * '; and appellant also points to the portion of Sec. 10 (a) (3) which

---

* Until a recent amendment legalizing this practice.
† *U. S. ex rel. Brandon* v. *Downer*, 135 Fed. Rep. 2nd Series 761. See pp. 35-36, "The Conscientious Objector and the Law."

75

refers to 'any officer * * * of the Army, Navy, Marine Corps, or Coast Guard * * * who may be assigned or detailed to any office or position to carry out the provisions of this Act (except to offices or positions on local boards, appeal boards, or agencies of appeal established or created pursuant to section 10 (a) (2) * * *).' He argues that the action of the President in delegating the power to pass on Presidential appeals to General Hershey violated those provisions of the Act. We need not pass upon that question. For Congress, on December 3, 1943, amended the pertinent portions of Sec. 10 (a) (2) to read 'civilian local boards, civilian appeal boards, and such other agencies, including agencies of appeal, as may be necessary. * * * Appeal boards within the Selective Service System shall be composed of civilians. * * *' It also then amended the pertinent portion of Sec. 10 (a) (3) by deleting the words 'agencies of appeal.' Assuming arguendo that the appeal was not properly considered under the statute as it read prior to this recent amendment, a reversal in the instant case on that ground would merely mean that General Hershey would now reconsider the matter with doubtless the same result. The question is therefore academic."

This is indeed a surprising argument. If there were an illegality in the procedure, the fact that the application of the correct procedure might produce no different result should not prevent a court from giving the registrant the benefit of due process of law, as who can tell that a reconsideration would necessarily produce the same result. The court indicated in its opinion that the decision in the Brandon case was wrong and it may well be that faced with this judicial guidance, General Hershey would have changed his opinion if Brandon had been allowed to have another appeal.

A quite different view from that of Judge Frank was taken by Chief Justice Groner of the United States Circuit Court of Appeals for the District of Columbia in the case of *Giese* v. *United States*.* The majority of the court had refused to go into the question of the validity of the Presidential appeal because they held that the registrant was not entitled to judicial review of his classification.† With this holding the Chief Justice disagreed and he went on to discuss the validity of the Presidential appeal. After quoting the statute Justice Groner states:

"Plainer words could hardly be found than are contained in these paragraphs to show that all appeals in all stages of the appeal must, except when the President acts personally, be determined by civilian citizens and not by the Army.

"The President, as he had the right to do, authorized, under certain conditions, an appeal to himself from a determination of a State board of appeal, and provided the method and time of taking such appeal. The regulation expressly declares that the local board 'shall not issue an order for a registrant to report for induction * * * during the period afforded * * * to take an appeal to the President or during the time such an appeal is pending'; and expressly declared that an order to report issued during either of the periods allowed shall be ineffective and shall be cancelled.

* * * * *

"From all of this it would seem to follow that if in the present instance the agency designated by the President to consider the appeal made to him is the 'agency of appeal' described in Section 10 (a) (2) of the Act, then by

---

* 143 Federal Reporter, 2nd Series, 633.
† The court based its holding on the case of *Falbo* v. *United States*, 320 United States Reports, 549, discussed in Chapter 11.

the very terms of the Act, it can be constituted only of civilians who are citizens of the United States. That it is such an agency of appeal seems too clear for argument, for, as we have seen, the Act contemplates the establishment of civilian local boards, appeal boards and agencies of appeal as the entire machinery covering the field of induction of citizens into the armed service. That this is correct is confirmed by the fact that after the indictment in this case and after General Hershey had been subpoenaed as a witness, Section 10 of the Act was amended so as thereafter to require civilian personnel only on local boards and State boards of appeal, and the Report of the House Committee shows that the amendment was considered necessary to assure Army and Navy personnel on the Presidential appeal board. I think it cannot be properly contended that the effect of the amendment was to give retroactive operation to the statute as amended. 'Retroactive declarations of legislative intent prejudicial to those who have acted under an earlier statute, whose construction seems clear, it would seem ought not to be implied * * *.' Haggar v. Helvering, 308 U. S. 389,400. Here, as I think, the original statute was clear. As a result of this amendment the law, as it now exists, permits such military personnel to act for the President, but it does not follow that because of it, as is suggested by counsel for the United States, if this case is reversed, Giese would be in precisely the same position he is in now. Obviously, this is incorrect, for Giese now faces prison if the judgment of the District Court is affirmed, whereas, if it is reversed, it by no means follows that when a proper board or lawful official delegated to act for the President has acted, Giese will not promptly obey the order to report for induction. But however that may be, the situation here must stand or fall upon the legality of what has happened and not upon what may. Hence it is that the decision ought to rest upon the determination whether, in the facts as shown in this record,

Giese violated the law. And if I am correct in thinking that his appeal has never been considered by a legal board and the order of induction made by the local board was prohibited by law until his appeal had been legally disposed of, it follows that the board's order was without effect; and this in turn results from the well established rule that a citizen may not be punished for the violation of the order of an executive officer or board, if it shall appear that the order was not within the authority of the officer or board. *Panama Refining Co.* v. *Ryan,* 293 U. S. 388; *Wichita R. & Light Co.* v. *Pub. U. Comm.,* 260 U. S. 48; *Morgan* v. *U. S.,* 298 U. S. 468, 304 U. S. 1.

All this is now past history since Congress has legalized the handling of Presidential appeals by military officers. However, the illegality of his handling of Presidential appeals will be marked in the history of this subject as a stain upon the record of the Director of Selective Service and this stain is rendered indelible by the Director's resort to Congress for legalization of this policy when it was attacked in the courts.

Chapter 14

Court Procedure

As POINTED OUT in Chapter 11, it is now possible for conscientious objectors to obtain judicial review without submitting to induction; otherwise the court procedure remains the same.

In *The Conscientious Objector and the Law*, reference was made to legislation for obtaining free copies of the stenographer's report of the testimony in appeals by poor defendants. Such a provision has now become law and is contained in a new section, Section 5a, of the Judicial Code entitled "Court Reporters"* which provides for the appointment by each district court of one or more court reporters and the payment by the United States of fees for transcripts of testimony in criminal or habeas corpus cases to persons allowed to sue, defend or appeal *in forma pauperis* (as poor persons).

As the writ of habeas corpus has been resorted to by many conscientious objectors, a brief discussion of the procedure may be helpful.

Any person held unlawfully in custody, as in prison, in the armed forces, or in a Civilian Public Service camp, may petition for a writ of habeas corpus, to the court having jurisdiction over the place of confinement. The petition may also be made by a friend or relative authorized by the person seeking release. If sufficient

---

* Chapter 3, Public Law 222, approved Jan. 20, 1944.

grounds for release from custody are shown on the face of the petition, the court must issue the writ, which is addressed to the respondent, that is to say, the person having custody of the petitioner, and will direct him to produce the petitioner in court. The writ must then be served on the respondent and proof of service filed with the clerk of the court.

On the return date, which will be specified in the writ, and at the place specified, the respondent must produce the petitioner before the court, and must also file a return to the writ, either admitting or denying the petitioner's charges. The court will then, if necessary, hold a hearing to inquire into the legality of the detention of the petitioner. This will be in the nature of a trial, but without a jury, being a civil, not a criminal matter.

Upon reaching a decision, the court will either sustain or dismiss the writ, and will enter an order either remanding the petitioner to custody, or directing his release. From this order an appeal may be taken.

Appendix

Excerpts from
Selective Service Regulations as Amended to
September 1, 1944

NOTE: Matter printed in italics has been added, and matter shown in brackets has been deleted, since September 1, 1943.

622.12 CLASS I-A-O: AVAILABLE FOR NONCOMBATANT MILITARY SERVICE; CONSCIENTIOUS OBJECTOR. In Class I-A-O shall be placed every registrant who would have been classified in Class I-A but for the fact that he has been found, by reason of religious training and belief [to be conscientiously opposed to participation in war in any form and] to be conscientiously opposed to combatant military service in which he might be ordered to take human life, but not conscientiously opposed to noncombatant military service in which he could contribute to the health, comfort, and preservation of others.

622.51 CLASS IV-E: AVAILABLE FOR WORK OF NATIONAL IMPORTANCE; CONSCIENTIOUS OBJECTOR. (a) In Class IV-E shall be placed every registrant who would have been classified in Class I-A but for the fact that he has been found, by reason of religious training and belief, to be conscientiously opposed to participation in war in any form and to be conscientiously opposed to both combatant and noncombatant military service.

(b) Upon being advised by the Director of Selective Service that a registrant who was inducted into the land or naval forces for military service will be discharged because of conscientious objections which make him unadaptable to military service, the local board shall change such registrant's

classification and place him in Class IV-E. The Director of
Selective Service shall assign such registrant to work of
national importance under civilian direction.

623.62 REGISTER OF CONSCIENTIOUS OBJECTORS. The local
board shall list on a register of conscientious objectors each
registrant whose claim for special classification as a conscientious objector has been sustained, either by the local board
or upon appeal. The register of conscientious objectors shall
show separately those registrants who have been classified as
available for noncombatant military service (Class I-A-O)
and those who have been classified as available for work of
national importance under civilian direction only (Class
IV-E). No special form is provided for this register.

627.14 TIME WHEN RECORD TO BE FORWARDED ON AP-
PEAL.* *(a) When an appeal is taken from the classification of
a registrant in Class I-A, Class I-A-O, or Class IV-E * * *
the file of the registrant shall be held by the local board
and shall not be forwarded to the board of appeal * * *
until (1) the registrant has been ordered to report for his
preinduction physical examination in the usual manner
when his order number is reached and (2) the results of the
preinduction physical examination have been received by
the local board or the registrant has failed to appear for his
preinduction physical examination at the time he is ordered
to do so. If as a result of the preinduction physical examination such registrant is found to be disqualified for service,
his classification shall be reopened and he shall be classified
in Class IV-F. In such cases the appeal will not be forwarded.*

627.25 SPECIAL PROVISIONS WHERE APPEAL INVOLVES CLAIM
THAT REGISTRANT IS A CONSCIENTIOUS OBJECTOR. (a) If an
appeal involves the question of whether or not a registrant
is entitled to be sustained in his claim that he is a conscientious objector, the board of appeal shall *take the following
action:*

---

* For a discussion of the effect of this amendment on conscientious
objectors, see page 74.

(1) First determine whether the registrant should be classified in one of the classes set forth in section 623.21 in the order set forth *except Class IV-F for physical or mental disability* and, if it so determines, it shall place the registrant in such class; *or*

(2) If it determines that the registrant should not be classified in one of the classes set forth in section 623.21 and the registrant has claimed classification in Class IV-E, determine whether to place the registrant in such class and, if it so determines, it shall place the registant in Class IV-E; or

(3) If it determines that the registrant should not be classified in one of the classes set forth in section 623.21 and the registrant has not claimed classification in Class IV-E but has claimed classification in Class I-A-O, determine whether to place the registrant in such class and, if it so determines, it shall place the registrant in Class I-A-O; or

(4) If it determines not to place such registrant in one of the classes set forth in section 623.21 *or in Class IV-E or in Class I-A-O* * * * it shall transmit the entire file to the United States Attorney for the judicial district in which the [local board of the registrant] *office of the board of appeal* is located for the purpose of securing an advisory recommendation from the Department of Justice [provided that in a case in which the local board has classified the registrant in Class IV-E or * * * Class I-A-O, the board of appeal may affirm the classification of the local board without referring the case to the Department of Justice]. No registrant's file shall be forwarded to the United States district attorney by any board of appeal and any file so forwarded shall be returned, unless in the "Minutes of Other Actions" on the Selective Service Questionnaire (Form 40) the record shows and the letter of transmittal states that the board of appeal reviewed the file and determined that the registrant should not be classified in one of the classes set forth in section 623.21 *(except Class IV-F for physical or mental disability) or in Class IV-E or Class I-A-O under the*

circumstances set forth in subparagraphs (1), (2), or (3) above.

(b) The Department of Justice shall thereupon make an inquiry and hold a hearing on the character and good faith of the conscientious objections of the registrant. The registrant shall be notified of the time and place of such hearing and shall have an opportunity to be heard. If the objections of the registrant are found to be sustained, the Department of Justice shall recommend to the board of appeal (1) that if the registrant is inducted into the land or naval forces, he shall be assigned to noncombatant service, or (2) that if the registrant is found to be conscientiously opposed to participation in such noncombatant service, he shall be assigned to work of national importance under civilian direction. If the Department of Justice finds that the objections of the registrant are not sustained, it shall recommend to the board of appeal that such objections be not sustained.

(c) Upon receipt of the report of the Department of Justice, the board of appeal shall determine the classification of the registrant, and in its determination it shall give consideration to, but it shall not be bound to follow, the recommendation of the Department of Justice. *The board of appeal shall place in the Cover Sheet (Form 53) of the registrant both the letter containing the recommendation of the Department of Justice and the report of the Hearing Officer of the Department of Justice.*

629.1 WHO WILL BE EXAMINED. *Every registrant, before he is ordered to report for induction, shall be given a preinduction physical examination * * * unless (1) he signs a Request for Immediate Induction (Form 219) or (2) he is a delinquent.*

643.1 PAROLE: GENERAL. Any person who has heretofore or may hereafter be convicted of a violation of any of the provisions of the Selective Training and Service Act of 1940, or any amendment thereto, or any rules or regulations prescribed thereunder, shall at any time after such conviction be eligible for parole for service in the land or naval

forces of the United States, or for work of national importance under civilian direction, or for any other special service established pursuant to said act, in the manner and
under the conditions hereinafter set out.

643.2 PAROLE OF PERSON REQUIRED TO REGISTER. The parole provided for in section 643.1 may be granted by the
Attorney General to any person required to register under
the provisions of the Selective Training and Service Act of
1940, as amended, and any proclamation of the President
thereunder, if in the judgment of the Attorney General it is
compatible with the public interest and the enforcement of
the Selective Training and Service Act of 1940, as amended,
upon the recommendation of the Director of Selective Service. Before recommending the parole of any such person,
the Director of Selective Service shall determine and include
in his recommendation whether such person should be paroled for (1) induction into the land or naval forces of the
United States; or (2) induction into the land or naval forces
of the United States for noncombatant service, as such service has been or may hereafter be defined; or (3) assignment
to work of national importance under civilian direction in
lieu of induction into the land or naval forces of the United
States; or (4) assignment to such other special service as may
be established by the Attorney General pursuant to the Selective Training and Service Act of 1940, as amended. If the
parole is granted, it shall conform to such recommendation.

[651.1 SELECTION OF REGISTRANTS FOR ASSIGNMENT TO
WORK OF NATIONAL IMPORTANCE. Every registrant who is
classified in Class IV-E, before he is assigned to work of
national importance under civilian direction, shall be given
a final-type physical examination for registrants in Class
IV-E. Each such registrant shall be ordered to report for
such examination when his order number is reached in the
process of selecting Class I-A and Class I-A-O registrants
to report for induction, provided his classification is not
under consideration on appearance, reopening, or appeal,

and the time in which he is entitled to request an appearance or take an appeal has expired.] *

652.14 PERIOD OF SERVICE. (a) A registrant in Class IV-E who has been assigned to a camp shall be engaged in work of national importance under civilian direction during the existence of any war in which the United States is engaged and during the six months immediately following the termination of any such war, unless sooner released under the same conditions as pertain in the armed forces.

(b) A person assigned to a camp on parole pursuant to part 643 shall be engaged in work of national importance under civilian direction for the length of the term of his sentence less deductions for good conduct as provided in part 643.

653.1 WORK PROJECTS. (a) The Director of Selective Service is authorized to establish, designate, or determine work of national importance under civilian direction. He may establish, designate, or determine, by an appropriate order, projects which he deems to be work of national importance. Such projects will be identified by number and may be referred to as "civilian public service camps."

(b) Each work project will be under the civilian direction of the United States Department of Agriculture, United States Department of the Interior, or such other Federal, State, or local governmental or private agency as may be designated by the Director of Selective Service. Each such agency will hereinafter be referred to as the "technical agency."

(c) The responsibility and authority for supervision and control over all [work] projects is vested in the Director of Selective Service.

653.2 CAMPS. (a) The Director of Selective Service may arrange for the establishment of a camp at any project

---

* Section 651.1 and other sections of Part 651 were deleted on January 1, 1944, when the new procedure for preinduction physical examinations was adopted, which rendered these sections obsolete. This section is printed here to show the nature of the change.

designated as work of national importance under civilian direction.

(b) Government-operated camps may be established in which the work of national importance and camp operations will both be under the civilian direction of a [Federal] technical agency using funds provided by the Selective Service System and operating under such camp rules as may be prescribed by the Director of Selective Service.

(c) The Director of Selective Service may authorize the National Service Board for Religious Objectors, a voluntary unincorporated association of religious organizations, to operate camps. The work project for assignees of such camps will be under the civilian direction of a technical agency. Such camps and work projects shall be operated under such camp rules as may be prescribed by the Director of Selective Service.

653.3   PROPERTY AND FINANCE.   (a) The Director of Selective Service will [allot funds to] *make available for* each technical agency having supervision over a work project *such funds as he may determine are required for the operation of camps * * *.* (NOTE: Accounting provisions are omitted.)

(b) The technical agency receiving property or equipment purchased from funds allotted by the Director of Selective Service shall designate a representative who shall be the responsible and the accountable officer.

(c) The National Service Board for Religious Objectors shall designate a representative as the responsible and accountable officer for and shall post a sufficient bond to indemnify the United States against loss of or damage to all camp buildings, camp-operating equipment, and other Government-owned property loaned to the non-Federal group in connection with the operation of any of its camps.

(d) When the National Service Board for Religious Objectors has been authorized to operate a camp, it shall assume the entire financial responsibility for the wages of the camp director and other employees, the clothing, feeding, housing, medical care, hospitalization, welfare, and recreation of assignees and all other costs of operating the camp. (NOTE: Subdivisions (e) and (f) providing for subsistence of assignees in Government-operated camps, or allowances in lieu thereof, and the expenses of operation of such camps are omitted.)

653.12 DUTIES. Assignees shall report to the camp to which they are assigned; remain therein until released or transferred elsewhere by proper authority, except when performing assigned duties or on authorized missions or leave outside of camp; perform their assigned duties promptly and efficiently; keep their persons, clothing, equipment, and quarters neat and clean; conserve and protect Government property; conduct themselves both in and outside of the camp so as to bring no discredit to the individual or the organization; and comply with such camp rules as may be prescribed or such directions as may be issued from time to time by the Director of Selective Service.

Index

CONSCIENCE AND THE STATE
Legal and Administrative Problems
of Conscientious Objectors, 1943-1944
By JULIEN CORNELL

THE TREATMENT of conscientious objectors presents a problem in democratic government which has not been fully solved. The areas in which progress has been made and the difficulties which still remain are a matter of concern not only to conscientious objectors themselves, but to all who cherish freedom of conscience and civil liberty.

In this volume, Julien Cornell outlines the legal and administrative position of conscientious objectors, and reviews the many changes which have occurred since he published *The Conscientious Objector and the Law*. This is not merely a supplement to the previous book, however, but is complete in itself.

The author, a New York lawyer and Counsel to the National Committee on Conscientious Objectors of the American Civil Liberties Union, has been continually occupied with the advice and defense of conscientious objectors during the past four years.   Price: $1.00

Also by Julien Cornell
The Conscientious Objector and the Law

FOR THOSE desiring a fuller discussion of the basic issues affecting conscientious objectors.

"This direct, plain, judicious report deserves the thoughtful reading of all Americans who are concerned about the maintenance of democratic principles even amid the anti-democratic pressures of war."—*From the preface by* HARRY EMERSON FOSDICK.

"Soberly and intelligently written, presents a case beyond dispute."—*Common Sense.*

"An interesting and provocative subject, presented clearly, eloquently and compactly."—*N. Y. Herald Tribune, "Books."*

158 Pages, Appendices, Index.   Cloth, $1.75

THE CONSCIENTIOUS OBJECTOR
AND THE LAW

The CONSCIENTIOUS OBJECTOR and the LAW

JULIEN CORNELL,
*Member of the New York Bar, Counsel to the
National Committee on Conscientious Objectors of the American Civil Liberties Union.*

Foreword by HARRY EMERSON FOSDICK

The John Day Company · New York

Distributors

Copyright, 1943, by Julien Cornell

Manufactured in the United States of America

TO THE MEMORY OF MY FATHER
EDWARD CORNELL
WHO LIVED BY THE LIGHT OF
HIS CONSCIENCE

Foreword

MR. CORNELL presents in this book an authoritative statement on the legal treatment of conscientious objectors in the United States during the present war. As special counsel on behalf of conscientious objectors, representing the American Civil Liberties Union's Committee, he has had both the opportunity and the obligation to know the facts at first hand. His direct, plain, judicious report deserves the thoughtful reading of all Americans who are concerned about the maintenance of democratic principles even amid the anti-democratic pressures of war.

Our treatment of conscientious objectors during this war has been unmistakably fairer than it was during the last war, but our gratification over that fact cannot be very enthusiastic in view of the facts presented in this book. We are far behind Great Britain in every aspect of our attitude toward, and treatment of, this special, unpopular minority. The law under which we operate is inadequate and was carelessly drawn, and its interpretation and enforcement have been needlessly confused and inconsistent, and in many instances downright unjust.

Whether the publication of this book can effect any modification of policy during this present conflict remains to be seen. There are level heads and sincerely democratic spirits endeavoring to meet with wisdom and fairness the puzzling problems that the conscientious objectors present. To them this book should be a welcome and useful statement of the facts concerning both our successes and our failures. And it may even remind others, if they can be persuaded to read it, that the most revealing criterion of a democracy is not the rule of the majority—to which even Hitler's dictatorship attained—but respect for the rights of minorities.

Whatever the immediate influence of this book, however, it is bound to be an historical document of continuing value. The facts here presented are an important part of the story of this war era and of what war does to the mind of a nation, even when it is fighting for democracy.

HARRY EMERSON FOSDICK.

Contents

ix

THE CONSCIENTIOUS OBJECTOR
AND THE LAW

Introduction

THE STORY of man's struggle for freedom of religious and intellectual belief is the story of civilization, for only as he becomes free does man enter that state superior to mere animal existence which may be truly called civilized. The measure of freedom of conscience afforded to those whose scruples prevent them from participating in war may, therefore, be regarded as a sort of metabolic test of the state of health of our civilization. If the nation can prosecute a war and at the same time give freedom to those who have conscientious objections to war, then our civilization is healthy and flourishing. But as conscientious objectors and other minorities are denied freedom, to that extent are we afflicted with the political disease which has destroyed Europe. This study is more, then, than a study of conscientious objection; it is a study of our government and our people, as tested by their treatment of a minority who place moral duties above duty to the State.

In order to understand the status of the conscientious objector, as defined under the law, it is necessary to understand his philosophy. This is perhaps best expressed in Christ's Sermon on the Mount, which contains the injunction "Resist not evil—love your enemies—do good to them that hate you." The conscientious objector, unlike most who call themselves Christians, adopts this central idea of Christian ethics; he believes these teachings, literally and completely. He makes no exception for the war which is waged to achieve good ends, since he believes that good ends may be reached only by doing good, not by the doing of evil. No matter what the cause in which it is fought, war is not only evil, but the epitome of evil, involving the destruction of human life, indeed the destruction of all moral and spiritual values. Living in the way of the spirit, which removes the occasion for all wars, the conscientious objector believes that when all men follow in this way there will be no more wars. He would leave warfare to the Hitlers, just as Jesus left to Caesar that which was Caesar's. Insisting on the use of moral means under all circumstances, the conscientious objector rejects the evil means of war, choosing rather to overcome evil with good.*

These principles, although they may be stated in different ways, are held by all conscientious objectors. But they use various means of giving effect to their principles. Most of them attempt to find some means of accomplishing social ends without the violence and destructiveness of warfare, by the doing of good instead of harm. The relief and welfare work of the American Friends Service Committee is a good example. Some pacifists follow the technique of non-cooperation developed by Gandhi, as a means of exerting political pressure compatible with pacifist principles. Some, it must be said, exhibit a negative attitude, opposing war without striving by other means to correct the ills which afflict our society.

---

* The point of view of the conscientious objector is expressed here in terms of Christian philosophy, although many conscientious objectors are not Christians, simply because Jesus expressed the pacifist idea more forcibly, perhaps, than anyone else.

These social and political attitudes may be important in themselves, but are not an infallible index by which the true conscientious objector may be distinguished from the charlatan. For the presence or absence of social and political attitudes commonly found among pacifists does not prove or disprove the existence of conscientious scruples. Even the non-cooperation of Gandhi is a method used extensively by non-pacifists, as it is today in the occupied countries of Europe.

The draft law being concerned with what a man conscientiously believes, we must search behind his actions for the principles from which actions spring. These principles will be much the same in all conscientious objectors; they are the principles of Christian morality, without which the conscientious objector believes that civilization cannot long endure.

Although his position is not generally understood, the pacifist has gained recognition for his steadfastness of purpose and his courage. Much of this has come through the good works of pacifists during and after the last war, when they lent succor to friend and foe alike. At last they are recognized officially as a minority entitled to their opinions. This is inherent in the present draft law, but was not so in the first World War, when Congress exempted from combatant service only those conscientious objectors who belonged to a religious sect whose creed opposed war. Most conscientious objectors then went to concentration camps, some were brutally treated, a few died under the manhandling which they received. In England a group was led before dawn onto a hilltop where they heard read an order that they should be shot at sunrise. The order was soon afterward revoked, but the men who heard it suffered a cruel torture. The brutality of the last war has not recurred in this one. For the present law recognizes the right of conscientious objectors to exemption because of conscience, not because of the accident of church membership. All who are conscientiously opposed to military service "by reason of religious training and belief" are exempted therefrom and required to perform as an alternative some form of "work of national importance under civilian direction."* In England, but not here, complete exemption may be had by those opposed to any form of service even under civilians. In both countries the claim of conscientious objection is carefully considered before the exemption is granted.

Thus the conscientious objector today may be, and often is, what his brothers of 1918 could not hope to be, a respected citizen doing his bit in accordance with his lights. The granting by law of this measure of self-respect to the conscientious objector is of inestimable importance, as he is no longer the unpatriotic slacker, but a respected citizen entitled, not perhaps to understanding, but at least to equal protection under the law.

All over the United States these men are bearing witness to their faith. At their own expense they are working at hard labor in the fields and forests, or in hospitals and research laboratories, under direction of technical agencies of the government, and in non-working hours under the care of three religious groups, the Quakers, the Mennonites, and the Brethren. These churches are represented by a single body, the National Service Board

---

* Sec. 5 g, Selective Training and Service Act of 1940.

for Religious Objectors, which operates as the agent of the government in maintaining the camps and other work projects. Over-all control is exercised by the Director of Selective Service. Although there are over 6000 men working, the government does not have to spend a penny, as all the expense is taken care of by the men themselves or by generous members of the churches involved.* Despite the stature to which the conscientious objector has grown, he is still not accorded in full measure the recognition which his legal and moral position deserves. Not only is he castigated by some sections of an intolerant public, but he frequently does not receive fair treatment at the hands of draft boards and public officials. The work projects have been in many ways badly handled, largely, it seems, because the Director of Selective Service would rather maintain good public relations with such critical groups as the American Legion than do what is best for the conscientious objectors. Normal progress and needed reform have been blocked time and again for no apparent reason, causing many conscientious objectors to leave the camps and enter prison. Draft boards and Selective Service officials have often been arbitrary, intolerant and sometimes bad tempered. Even the courts have been slow to protect the rights of the conscientious objector. On the other hand, prosecuting officials have usually been sympathetic and helpful, as have officials of the Bureau of Prisons.

With this background the various ways in which the law impinges on the conscientious objector may be better understood.

---

* All permanent equipment, however, is furnished by the government.

How the Draft Law Was Written

To THE MISFORTUNE of the nation's young manhood, and especially of its conscientious objectors, the Selective Training and Service Act was rushed through Congress although the war clouds were still far away on the horizon. The conscience clause was hurriedly drafted with but slight consideration by congressional committees, and no consideration at all on the floor of Congress. As a result, there are many inadequacies in the provision which emerged which might have been avoided with a little time and care, especially if any attention had been given to the British law and experience under it.

The original draft of the Burke-Wadsworth Bill, as it was called, contained a provision for conscientious objectors copied almost verbatim from the 1917 draft law, which exempted from combatant service only members of certain pacifistic religious sects.* But the narrowness of the exemption brought protests from such men as Harry Emerson Fosdick, Roswell P. Barnes and Howard K. Beale, who testified before congressional committees regarding the unfortunate treatment accorded to conscientious objectors in the first World War under the similar statute, the desire of the Army that this problem not again be thrust upon it by failure of Congress to provide adequate exemptions, the large number of conscien-

---

* H.R. 10132, 76th Congress, 3rd Session, Sec. 7 (d).

tious objectors as compared with the tiny fraction who would qualify for the proposed exemption, and the successful operation of the British law which provides exemptions, some conditional, some absolute, for all conscientious objectors, no matter what their religious views, and also provides for a separate register for conscientious objectors so that those who object to any compliance with conscription, even to that extent, need not register for the draft.*

Various amendments were offered to improve the bill, but the amendment which was finally adopted was offered by two Quakers, Paul French and Raymond Wilson, and defines conscientious objection as follows:

"Nothing contained in this Act shall be construed to require any person to be subject to combat training or service in the land or naval forces of the United States who, by reason of religious training and belief, is conscientiously opposed to participation in war in any form, and is found to be a bona fide objector as hereinafter provided."†

The identical wording appears in the law as enacted, except that the portion following the last comma was dropped. There can be no question, then, as to the source of the provisions in the law, and what light can be shed on the meaning of Congress is to be found in the testimony of French and Wilson before the House Committee on Military Affairs, plus a single brief reference on the floor of Congress.‡ This legislative history of the statute helps to clear up some of the ambiguities, particu-

---

* See Hearings before the Committees on Military Affairs, 76th Congress, 3rd Session: House of Representatives on H.R. 10132; Senate, on S. 4164.

† Hearings on H.R. 10132, pages 201 to 211.

‡ Congressional Record, 76th Congress, 3rd Session, page 10106.

larly the meaning of the troublesome phrase "religious training and belief."*

In addition to the ambiguous religious test which is imposed, the law contains other major defects. Chief of these is the failure to provide total exemption for those who cannot accept any form of service under conscription. (In England total exemption may be had by those who have conscientious scruples against any form of service, and has been granted to six per cent of those claiming to be conscientious objectors.) The requirement that conscientious objectors register with other draftees was foolish, as it could have been foreseen, had any study been given to the matter, that many would refuse to register. This difficulty was known to the framers of the amendment referred to above, and they proposed that a separate register of conscientious objectors be provided. This had the approval of the War Department, which helped to frame the amendment, but was dropped for some unknown reason before final passage. Here, again, the British model would have served as a valuable guide, but those responsible for the final wording of the bill ignored it, and apparently ignored also the wishes of the War Department.

Because of their blundering, these unknown draftsmen have sent scores of young men to prison who would under a clause such as that contained in the British law, be recognized as conscientious objectors.

Perhaps more important than any of these was the failure to provide proper tribunals to consider claims of conscience. The British wisely provide for the appoint-

* See Chapter 2.

ment of judges to head the tribunals and also allow rights to the conscientious objector similar to those which he has in a court of law, as shown in Chapter 17. In sharp contrast to the excellent record of the British tribunals is the deplorable attitude of many of our local boards, which frequently either refuse to recognize claims of conscientious objection at all, or admit their inability to solve such problems, and pass the buck to the appeal boards. The system of investigations and hearings by the F. B. I. and a "hearing officer" might have worked if proper procedure had been set up instead of the "Star Chamber" sort of proceeding for which the Regulations provide.*

Not only is the system execrable, but the men chosen as hearing officers have in general been badly chosen, as many of them not only have no acquaintance with or understanding of the pacifist position, but have had no experience whatever in handling the human and psychological problems which are involved. Some of the decisions of these men are founded on a complete misapprehension of the philosophy of pacifism, or on absurdities of logic. At least one such decision has been reversed in the courts because of its patent absurdity.†

Despite the foregoing shortcomings, and they are most serious as shown by the fact that about 2000 conscientious objectors have been imprisoned, one of the main features of the law has worked well on the whole. This is the provision for work of national importance under civilian direction. Administered by religious agencies

---

* Selective Service Regulations, paragraph 627.25.
† The decision in the *Randolph Phillips* case, referred to in Chapter 7.

and technical agencies of the government, the system has been largely satisfactory, but the cost to the churches has been heavy; they and the conscientious objectors who can support themselves will have spent about $4,000,000 at the end of the year 1943, and the government will have spent nothing, merely lending equipment.*

The Director of Selective Service has prevented proper development of maintenance projects affording work of real importance, insisting on keeping most of the men in camps of the C. C. C. type, although they are urgently needed on farms, in hospitals, and in training for relief and reconstruction after the war. But these faults are due to the rigidity of an administration dominated by military men and not to any defect in the law itself.

---

* The government has recently, however, set up a camp at Mancos, Colorado, the expense of which will be borne from the appropriation for Selective Service.

2.

The Religious Test of Conscientious Objection

UNDER OUR DRAFT LAW exemption from military service is granted to those who can show that they are conscientiously opposed to participation in all war and in addition that they are so opposed "by reason of religious training and belief." The statute itself so requires.* In judging professed conscientious objectors, therefore, not only is the genuineness of the claim examined, but also the religious test required by the law must be applied. It is not a difficult matter to distinguish between the man of conscience and the fraud, but who can say with any certainty that a man has or does not have religion? Is he who attends a church religious? Does he who subscribes to an accepted theology thereby become religious? And if more than this is implied in the term religious, then what are its confines?

These are questions which must be resolved before the religious test can fairly be put to a conscientious objector. Because these questions have not been faced, and because of a lack of religious tolerance on the part of public officials and draft boards, several hundred sincere young men have been imprisoned. Most of these men belong to no church and subscribe to no creed, but are deeply imbued with a love for humanity which makes them reject war. If they are not religious, then religion has sunk

---

* Section 5 g, Selective Training and Service Act of 1940.

low indeed. And the most shocking aspect of this situation is that the decisions denying such men exemption as conscientious objectors have been uniformly reviewed and upheld by Selective Service Headquarters at Washington where a group of army officers sitting as a Presidential Appeal Board has consistently rejected appeals on the apparent theory that the religious test has not been satisfied. This board of army officers has shown by its decisions in these cases, that they regard men without ecclesiastical and theological connections as lacking in "religion" thereby condemning them to rot in prison, while the veriest hypocrite who happens to belong to a church readily gains exemption from military service by reciting the commandment "Thou shalt not kill." Can it be that Congress intended such an unhappy result? I think not.

The congressional history of the statute indicates that the religious test was inserted in the law with the idea of withholding exemption from persons motivated by political or personal ends, particularly Communists. The original draft of the Burke-Wadsworth bill followed the 1917 draft law and exempted only those belonging to pacifist sects. As stated in Chapter 1, witnesses testified at the committee hearings in protest against the narrowness of the proposed exemption. The result was amendment, which was drawn by two Quakers, Raymond Wilson and Paul French, at a conference with a Colonel O'Keliher of the War Department. The amendment which they drew was accepted by the Senate Committee and quickly written into law. The meaning which the framers of this provision attached to the term "religious" may be discovered from their testimony before the congressional committees, which makes it plain that they intended to provide exemption for conscientious objection based upon deep and sincere conviction, but not for objections based on political or social expediencies. They used the word "religious" to describe convictions so woven into the philosophy of the individual as to become his religion, which he lives by and would lay down his life for. Perhaps the word "conscientious" standing alone would have expressed the meaning better, but the War Department, and Congress also, were probably afraid that this would let in political objectors, who might be conscientious, but surely could never be described as religious in their attitude.

It was not long before the hearing officers charged with passing on claims of conscientious objectors had to decide what was meant by the religious test. One of these officers wrote to the Attorney General for advice, who in turn took the matter up with General Lewis B. Hershey, Director of Selective Service. The result was an opinion by General Hershey that his office would insist as a part of the test of conscientious objection that the objector recognize "some source of all existence which is divine because it is the source of all things."* Now this would require belief not only in a deity, but also in a deity which is the creator of the universe. In this age of skepticism there are many sincere conscientious objectors who do not have a belief in such a deity, although they are far from the sort of political objector whom Congress sought to exclude from the benefit of the exemption.

* Letter to Department of Justice dated March 5, 1942.

These men are in prison. And in addition, men who although they are believers in a deity have no church connections, and subscribe to no formal creed are frequently denied exemption under the construction of the religious test which prevails with General Hershey and his aides, especially if they have ever given political expression to their pacifism, even though the religious motivation is primary.

When a conscientious objector is examined, he is always asked what church he belongs to, what creed he subscribes to, and what sort of a god he believes in. If he is not orthodox in these matters, he is usually denied exemption on the ground that he is not religious, despite evidence of humanitarian and moral views which might well be termed religious. The test is applied narrowly, and without regard to the broad purpose of the law to grant exemption to conscientious scruples so long as they are not political.

The responsibility for the deplorable state of affairs which sends noble men to prison because they are unorthodox in religious matters rests primarily with the Director of Selective Service, who has the power, through presidential appeals, to control the tenor of decisions by the draft boards and the hearing officers. Since appeals to the Director have proved fruitless, resort has been had to the courts.

The first case involving this issue was that of Mathias Kauten, who was examined by Lamar Hardy as hearing officer and found to be sincere, but lacking in religion because he was a professed atheist. The evidence was clear, however, that he was a man of unusual character,

an artist, sensitive, quiet, and with a sense of the brother-
hood of man which led him to refuse to kill. After losing in the trial court on the criminal charge of failure to
appear for induction, Kauten won from the United
States Circuit Court of Appeals in New York a decision
that the humanitarian views of a conscientious objector
are the proper test for exemption, not his theological
beliefs. The court said:

"The provisions of the present statute take into account
the characteristics of a skeptical generation and make the
existence of a conscientious scruple against war in any
form, rather than allegiance to a definite religious group
or creed, the basis of exemption. * * * A compelling voice
of conscience * * * we should regard as a religious impulse. * * *

It is unnecessary to attempt a definition of religion; the
content of the term is found in the history of the human
race and is incapable of compression into a few words.
Religious belief arises from a sense of the inadequacy of
reason as a means of relating the individual to his fellow-
men and to his universe—a sense common to men in the
most primitive and in the most highly civilized societies.
It accepts the aid of logic but refuses to be limited by it.
It is a belief finding expression in a conscience which
categorically requires the believer to disregard elementary
self-interest and to accept martyrdom in preference to
transgressing its tenets.

* * * * *

There is a distinction between a course of reasoning
resulting in a conviction that a particular war is inexpedi-
ent or disastrous and a conscientious objection to participation in any war under any circumstances. The latter,
and not the former, may be the basis of exemption under
the Act. The former is usually a political objection, while
the latter, we think, may justly be regarded as a response

of the individual to an inward mentor, call it conscience or God, that is for many persons at the present time the equivalent of what has always been thought a religious impulse."*

After this very satisfactory statement of the meaning of the religious test, the court went on to decide that the defense could not be raised, in a prosecution for failure to report for induction, for reasons which are discussed in Chapter 6.

This opinion is of capital importance, because the court rejects the archaic notion prevalent in Selective Service headquarters that religious scruples must stem from a church, a creed, or at least a belief in God. In the court's view, the promptings of conscience are essentially religious in character, even though church, creed, and God are all denied. Regarded in this light, the word "religious" as used in the law merely emphasizes the term conscience, as meaning the compelling voice of some inward spiritual guide rather than a mere conviction based on intellectual judgment or expediency. A true conscientious scruple in this sense, says the court, justifies exemption under the draft law, and is religious in character, for conscience is itself a religious voice.

This interpretation of the law avoids the pitfall into which the draft officials have fallen. They have felt obliged to insist that mere conscience alone is not enough for exemption, in addition there must be some religious element added to conscience, because the law contains the word religious as well as the word conscientious. This dilemma, which is merely a logistic

----

* Augustus N. Hand, Circuit Judge, in *United States* v. *Mathias Kauten,* 133 Federal Reporter, 2nd Series, page 708.

dilemma, the court has resolved by pointing out that true conscience is religious in nature. The word religious in the law, then, merely clarifies the meaning of the term conscientious, but does not impose any additional requirement for exemption. The similarity between Judge Hand's attitude toward religion and the attitude of the Quakers, perhaps best known of pacifist groups, is so striking as to call for comment. "A compelling voice of conscience," he writes, is "a religious impulse," and he refers to "an inward mentor, call it conscience or God." The Quakers believe that every man has within him something divine, which is variously called conscience or Inner Light, and that man by calling upon the spiritual resources within himself may commune not only with other men, they too being spiritual in 'essence, but also with the divine spirit which dwells within us all. It is this very belief in the spiritual nature of man that leads Quakers like most pacifists to refuse to take human life, and it is therefore appropriate that response to the voice of conscience, or God, within the human breast should be sufficient cause for exemption as a conscientious objector. With rare insight, Judge Hand has caught the essence of pacifist philosophy and clarified the intention of Congress, which was undoubtedly responsive to that same philosophy although not so clearly expressed.

Despite the broad definition of the words "religious training and belief" in the *Kauten* case, draft boards and Selective Service officials continue in many cases to use a narrow construction as before. General Hershey has not indicated that he agrees with the court's ruling, which is in sharp contradiction of his own earlier pronouncement, and the appeals to the President, which he decides, continue to be decided on narrow grounds.

The present interpretation which General Hershey places upon the phrase "religious training and belief" is revealed in the second report of his administration of the Selective Training and Service Act entitled "Selective Service in Wartime" which covers the year following Pearl Harbor, and was submitted to the President in August, 1943. In this report General Hershey writes:

"The conscientious objection recognized in the statute is conscientious objection based on religious training and belief. Objections, based on the futility or stupidity of war or on grounds of a social or economic or merely humanitarian character, are not recognized by the law. * * * There may be nobility and intelligence in these points of view but they are not within the scope of the law.

"The sincerity of such beliefs in itself is not a basis for deferment, though a registrant to be deferred on religious grounds must be sincere in his beliefs. The only grounds on which conscientious objections to war may result in deferred classes are religious training and belief. * * *"

"The appeals of conscientious objectors have presented some of the most troublesome as well as the most interesting questions. Here divergent ideas broke sharply over that rock of contention presented by the congressional language 'religious training and belief.' Local boards and boards of appeal generally brought little sympathy to the consideration of these cases. * * * Many board members held the view that such objection must arise from religious training and belief in those particular religious organizations which make objection to war a definite part of their creed. It was argued, for example, that a member of the Catholic Church could not possibly have a basis for conscientious objections.

"Hearing officers of the Department of Justice took a somewhat broader but still limited view in their early reports. They generally held that the conviction, while limited to no particular creed, must nevertheless rest upon an easily recognizable religious background with the definition of religion the usual somewhat formal concept.

"After much consideration we adopted a more liberal view, based upon the conclusion that the definitions of religion and the variety of religious experience are so nearly infinite in number as to make futile any attempt to say whether this or that one met the law. The practical effect of this decision was to say that conscientious convictions held by a man reared in the environment of a religious civilization and exposed, if only subjectively, to its ethical concepts, have their roots in the same soil from which spring religious convictions, and furnish evidence from which may be drawn the inference that he recognizes a Deity or a power above and beyond the human. This view has prevailed."

Apparently General Hershey clings to the idea that belief in a deity is the essence of the religious motivation required by the law, and that a conscience prompted by humanitarian or moral concepts is not religious, although the court in the *Kauten* case ruled that any conscientious scruple, even of an atheist, which was not based on political or personal expediency, should be regarded as a religious impulse.

Because of General Hershey's rulings on the definition of the term "religious training and belief," cases are still being taken into court on this question. But narrow decisions are still to be expected so long as narrow-minded men have power to expound the law, and the courts refuse to review their decisions.

3.

Classification Procedure

THERE ARE THREE classifications under the draft regulations for those who are not deferred from service: I-A, full military service, and I-A-O and IV-E for conscientious objectors. I-A-O is the class for conscientious objectors who are willing to serve in the army in non-combatant capacities, while IV-E is reserved for those who will serve only in civilian capacities.

When he files his questionnaire, the conscientious objector must fill out Series X which contains this statement:

"By reason of religious training and belief I am conscientiously opposed to war in any form and for this reason request that the Local Board furnish me a Special Form for Conscientious Objector (Form 47) which I am to complete and return to the Local Board."

Previously under Series X it was required that an agreement be signed to perform any service which might be assigned. Many were unwilling to agree in advance to perform any service to which they might be assigned and accordingly limited their answers by stipulating that they would perform only such service as their conscientious scruples would permit. This requirement has now been withdrawn.

Upon filing the questionnaire with Series X filled out, the draft board usually sends to the registrant the special form for conscientious objectors, Form 47, but if the draft board does not send this form, the registrant must obtain and file it, since the burden is imposed upon him by the regulations of stating the basis for his claim of conscientious objection on this form. Form 47 includes these questions:

"1. Describe the nature of your belief which is the basis of your claim.
 2. Explain how, when, and from whom or from what source you received the training and acquired the belief which is the basis of your claim.
 3. Give the name and present address of the individual on whom you rely most for religious guidance.
 4. Under what circumstances, if any, do you believe in the use of force?
 5. Describe the actions and behavior in your life which in your opinion most conspicuously demonstrate the consistency and depth of your religious convictions.
 6. Have you ever given public expression, written or oral, to the views herein expressed as the basis for your claim? If so, specify when and where.
 7. Have you ever been a member of any military organization or establishment?
 8. Are you a member of a religious sect or organization?
 9. Describe carefully the creed or official statements of said religious sect or organization as it relates to participation in war.
 10. Describe your relationships with and activities in all organizations with which you are or have been affiliated other than religious or military."

These questions may evoke ready answers from one whose pacifism stems from the formal teachings of his church. However, most conscientious objectors do not parrot what they have learned, but hold their views as a result of individual thinking. Many belong to no church, and many who do belong find in the church no basis for conscientious objection. For these, the religious basis is entirely a personal one, and they cannot therefore adequately express their stand by answering the questions as given in the form. It is necessary to expand somewhat the scope of the questions by stating the nature and source of religious basis for conscientious objection, although it may be unconnected with any church, creed, or theological belief.

Many are puzzled how to answer question number two, as they may rely only on themselves for religious insight. Most Quakers, for example, worship God directly and rely on no priest or religious mentor for guidance. Yet if a flat "No" is given for answer, this may be construed as implying lack of religion. It is therefore necessary to explain the source of religious inspiration, if there be no personal guide upon whom the individual relies.

The fourth question is a "catch" question. Of course, everyone but an anarchist believes that force is necessary in human affairs to control criminal elements, but this has nothing to do with the use of force for the killing of innocent people in warfare.

The fifth question may bother a modest individual, but he can at least claim to be honest and loving in his daily life.

The sixth question is also troublesome, as most pacifists are not given to discussing their views in public.

The ninth question would appear to be out of keeping with the nature of the inquiry, as the personal views of the registrant are under examination, not the creeds of his church, which he may not believe in whether or not he subscribes to them officially.

On the basis of the answers to the questions in Form 47, the local board proceeds to determine whether the claim of conscientious objection should be allowed. If the board so desires, it may call the registrant before it for personal questioning, but this is usually not done. When the decision is reached, a notice of classification is sent to the registrant. He has ten days from the date of mailing of the notice within which to appeal. During this ten-day period he may file a written request for a hearing, if he has not already had one. This extends the time to appeal to ten days from the date set for the hearing. The board must grant the request, and at the hearing the registrant may not only present his views orally, but may also offer witnesses in his behalf, and put into the record any evidence which may be needed to complete the file. This is his last chance to make out a complete case, as he cannot later on introduce any further evidence, unless he can persuade the local board, in its discretion, to re-open the case.

After the hearing, a second notice of classification is sent, which the registrant may appeal if he is still unsatisfied.

Frequently local boards have failed to give proper consideration to conscientious objectors. Many boards do not understand the problems involved, have not studied the law, are angry and intolerant, or simply lack the necessary mental and moral equipment for such a delicate task. Early in the history of the draft law it was realized that the local boards were totally unsuited to the job of classifying conscientious objectors, which should never have been entrusted to such lay groups, chosen hurriedly and without reference to their qualifications for this phase of their work. The sensible way to handle the problem would have been to set up fewer tribunals, as in England, and man them with men specially chosen for their ability and experience at analyzing human behavior.

Because of the inadequacy of the local boards, it was found necessary to take away from the boards the power to send conscientious objectors into the army by denying their claims in cases where appeals were not properly taken. This was done by the Director of Selective Service issuing instructions that cases where a claim of conscientious objection was involved should, if the local board denied the claim, be appealed even where the registrant asked for an appeal after the time to appeal had expired, or otherwise departed from the prescribed procedure. Many failed to appeal in fear or ignorance, or appealed too late, and were faced with induction into the army although they had never been given any real consideration. The granting of appeals in such cases went a long way toward correcting the situation by taking the matter out of the hands of the local board. It would have been far better, however, to have provided special boards for these cases, abolishing the power of the regular boards to determine claims of conscientious objectors. Here again the trouble may be traced to hasty and poor draftsmanship of the regulations. A little study of the British experience would have demonstrated the error of allowing lay boards to decide these problems.

The procedure on appeal is far better. First the file is sent to the appeal board, which decides whether any ground appears for deferment, for dependency, occupation or otherwise. If not, the appeal board transmits the file to the United States Attorney for the district, who turns the case over to the Federal Bureau of Investigation. A confidential and thorough investigation is made by the F. B. I. and a report prepared which is handed up to a hearing officer, specially appointed as an Assistant to the Attorney General for the hearing of these cases. There is one hearing officer for each Federal judicial district, and in the larger cities there are several. These men are usually attorneys of mature years and wide experience.

The hearing officer after examining the file holds a hearing at which the registrant is given an opportunity to explain his position, and may present witnesses or documentary evidence. (This is generally received, although the regulations do not provide for introduction of new evidence at this stage.) It is highly desirable to have witnesses present to testify to the good character and sincerity of the registrant, and to present letters or affidavits from any witnesses who cannot attend, if for no other reason simply because failure to do so is invariably commented upon by the hearing officer in his written report of the hearing. The hearings are conducted in an informal and friendly manner. The personal bearing of the registrant is perhaps his most valuable evidence, since no proof of sincerity is better than simple honesty and truthfulness, which shows itself in the bearing of one who is entirely sincere.

While the hearings are conducted with thoroughness and decorum, they fail to meet the most elementary requirements of constitutional procedure. The defendant in any trial at law is entitled to be confronted by the witnesses against him, to hear the evidence against him, to have counsel in his defense, to have an opportunity to rebut the evidence by his own witnesses, and to be judged by a jury of his peers. No pillar of our constitution, indeed of Anglo-American law, is more firmly planted than the requirement of a fair trial by strict adherence to these rights of defendants. But in the hearing given to a conscientious objector he is denied all of these fundamental rights, and in truth is denied a fair hearing. He is not confronted with the witnesses against him, he does not even know who they are; he does not have access to the F. B. I. report containing the evidence against him, which is not even placed in his Selective Service file and is withheld also from the appeal board; he is not allowed to have counsel, and therefore may present a poor case simply through youth and inexperience; he cannot rebut damaging evidence in the F. B. I. report because he is not even told of it; and finally he is judged by a single individual, human and fallible, despite the cardinal principle of our jurisprudence granting the right of trial by jury rather than by a single judge.

In these respects the hearing procedure is unjust, and has in many cases resulted in injustice. Especially deplorable is the "Star Chamber" character of the whole proceeding. The F. B. I. report is secret, available only to the hearing officer. Not even a court reviewing his actions will see this report, as it is not placed in the file.

The hearing is not public, no counsel is allowed, and instead of a tribunal one man sits in judgment, deciding upon evidence which is not disclosed. It need hardly be pointed out that such autocratic procedures violate principles of justice long established in Anglo-American law.

Here the blame must be laid at the door of the bureaucratic philosophy which pervades Washington. The men who drew up this procedure are no doubt like many in the government enamored of the idea that administrative boards can better decide quasi-judicial matters by dictatorial methods than can the clumsy and slow procedures required by our law and constitution for judicial procedure. The due process of the law may be slow, and it may be clumsy, but it has a solidity and a democracy which is all too lacking in the proceedings of the administrative boards of the New Deal.

After concluding the hearing, the hearing officer writes an opinion in which he reviews the evidence. The report then concludes with a statement as to the man's sincerity and a recommendation that his claim be sustained or that it be denied.

This report, with the rest of the file, but without either the F. B. I. report or the minutes of the hearing, is transmitted to the appeal board. Having before it only the findings of the hearing officer, and not the evidence on which he based these findings, the appeal board hardly has any basis on which to disagree with him, and in most cases concurs in the conclusion of the hearing officer. This ends the case. The registrant has no right of further appeal. He will receive a notice of classification and then if his claim is sustained, a notice to report to a camp for conscientious objectors, and if it is denied, a notice to report for induction.

In order to correct errors, and to promote uniform policy, the state Director of Selective Service or the national Director of Selective Service may appeal in behalf of the registrant from the decision of the appeal board. This appeal is taken to the President, who has delegated the authority to hear such appeals to the Director of Selective Service. The registrant has no right to such an appeal, but in order to exhaust all his remedies, he should write to the national and state directors immediately following an unfavorable decision from the appeal board and request them to take an appeal in his behalf to the President.

If such a request is made, the file will be reviewed either by the state or national director's office, and if it is thought that an injustice has been done an appeal will be taken. The review given is very sketchy, however. For a time such requests were automatically denied without any investigation whatever. This shocking practice came to the attention of General Hershey, it is said, when he called for the file in a case where representations had been made to him by friends of the registrant. He learned that the file was not in the office, and that one of his aides had refused to take an appeal without even having taken the trouble to examine the file.

If the appeal to the President is accepted, which happens all too seldom, the matter is considered by a board of army officers appointed for this purpose by General Hershey. Presumably these officers make recommendations to the General which he "rubber stamps" in the name of the President. There is serious doubt whether it is legal for army officers to decide these appeals, as the draft law requires all such matters to be handled by civilians.* This question is discussed in the next chapter.

With the decision on presidential appeal, if any, and otherwise with the decision of the appeal board, the classification process ends.

---

* Section 10 (a) (2), Selective Training and Service Act of 1940.

4.

Presidential Appeals

ALTHOUGH APPEALS to the President are allowed by the
draft law as of right only in a few instances, the state
or national Director of Selective Service may appeal
to the President at any time from any determination
of a draft board.* Many such appeals have been taken
by the Director of Selective Service in order to control
the draft boards, and infuse into their decisions some
degree of uniformity. The appeal to the President,
therefore, occupies somewhat the same position in the
scheme of draft classifications as appeals to the Supreme
Court in our judicial system.

Particularly in conscientious objector cases has the
device of appeal to the President by the Director of
Selective Service been used. In fact, every decision by
an appeal board is reviewed in Washington to determine
whether an appeal should be taken to the President if
the conscientious objector requests it. And whether
or not such request is made, the Department of Justice
always reviews the opinions and recommendations of
hearing officers. If unsatisfactory they can be corrected
by voluntary revision of the hearing officer or by appeal
to the President.

Although when an appeal is requested the file is reviewed in each case, very seldom does the Director of

---

* Selective Service Regulations, paragraph 628.1.

Selective Service grant the request, and when he does take an appeal it is rarely successful, even in cases having real merit. The Director of Selective Service has failed to achieve uniformity of policy toward conscientious objectors, because of inadequate use of presidential appeals.

Perhaps the chief trouble with presidential appeals is that they are decided by military officers. Not only did the President delegate to the Director of Selective Service, a military officer, the authority for deciding these appeals, but the Director shares his responsibility in this regard with five other military officers, all wearing uniform and on active duty, who act as a board to decide all presidential appeals, subject to formal approval by the Director. That the real decisions are made by the military officers is apparent from the fact that over 21,000 such appeals have been decided. The Director could not have given much personal attention to that many appeals.

The Selective Training and Service Act provides that the President shall provide for classification of drafted men by establishing "civilian local boards and such other civilian agencies, including appeal boards and agencies of appeal, as may be necessary."* There can be no doubt that the board which decides presidential appeals, as well as General Hershey himself, is either an appeal board or an agency of appeal, and there can be no doubt that the law requires these functions to be performed by civilians.

This is a serious illegality. The law wisely requires

_____
* Section 10 (a) (2).

that civilians control the vital matter of classification. Military methods are not suitable. Yet the Director of Selective Service has chosen a board entirely composed of military men to perform this task. The dangers which the law was designed to prevent have occurred. The military officers, however painstaking they may be in their job, have dealt with conscientious objectors out of the background of military experience. Perhaps this is the reason why such questions as the defining of the religious requirement for conscientious objectors have been decided narrowly and strictly.

Not only are presidential appeals decided illegally by military officers, but they are decided in autocratic fashion. There is no hearing, no evidence is received, no brief submitted by the claimant, the government's representatives act as prosecutor as well as judge and jury, and to top it all no opinions are written so that it is impossible for the claimant to find out why his claim has been denied, as it almost always is. This may be permissible in court martial, which these officers are accustomed to, but it is not the sort of procedure which one expects in a civil proceeding, nor the sort of procedure which the Congress expected the President to provide for by requiring him to appoint civilian appeal boards and civilian agencies of appeal.

In view of the attack which is here made on General Hershey's action in setting up the board of presidential appeal and staffing it with military men, it is only fair to let him explain himself. The following is taken from a press release of the War Manpower Commission dated January 6, 1943, which quotes General Hershey:

"The law provides that appeal boards must be set up. Beyond these boards is the right of appeal, under some conditions by the registrant, in all cases by State Directors of Selective Service to the President.

"On December 23, 1940, the President delegated to the Director of Selective Service his authority to perform all the functions and duties vested in the Selective Service law that relate to appeals from the determination of boards of appeal. This authority was transferred to the Chairman of the War Manpower Commission, by Executive Order of December 5, 1942, but soon after was re-delegated to me by Chairman Paul V. McNutt of War Manpower Commission. So that I, as Director of Selective Service, might act upon these appeals I set up in the Selective Service System a board of review to consider presidential appeals and make recommendations to me concerning them. It has no authority to make final decisions regarding them. The board to date has handled approximately 15,000 cases.

"This board of review is headed by Colonel John D. Langston, of North Carolina, who was admitted to the North Carolina bar in 1905. Colonel Langston was in charge of the draft in North Carolina from December 1917 to September 1918, when he was transferred to Washington where he served as chief of the Classification and Deserter Division of the Provost Marshal General's Department. Although he went back to private life after the World War, he was recalled to active military duty in 1940, and assigned to National Headquarters of the Selective Service System. Colonel Langston was awarded the Distinguished Service Medal for his work in connection with manpower mobilization in the World War.

"Lt. Col. Raymond T. Higgins, of Washington, D. C., who serves with Colonel Langston, has been actively engaged in Selective Service work for nearly 25 years. Not only did he serve in the World War, but he participated in all of the deliberations of the Joint Army and Navy

Selective Service law. Colonel Higgins was on duty in the Office of the Assistant Chief of Staff, G-1, in a civilian capacity from 1927 to 1930 assisting in the preparation of the Selective Service plans and has acted as an instructor in the conduct of Army extension courses for the Specialist Group for Selective Service.

"Lt. Col. Gordon Snow, of Salt Lake City, Utah, another member, organized the draft in Salt Lake City in 1917, was made a captain in 1918, and was named Draft Executive for the State of Utah in 1918, a post in which he served until 1919.

"Major Roy L. Deal, of North Carolina, a former judge in the State, served in the classification division of the Provost Marshal General's Department in the World War under General Enoch H. Crowder, and thus has a long experience in Selective Service matters.

"Major Roscoe S. Conkling, was director of the draft in New York City in the World War.

"To my mind these men are unusually competent, and by their training and experience are highly qualified to review appeals, both from the standpoint of the registrant and the Nation in this time of war. I am confident that any recommendations which they make are based on sound judgment, a thorough understanding of the facts, a high regard for individual rights and the general welfare."

Representations have been made to the Director of Selective Service in an effort to have the military board replaced by civilians. He has refused to do so, saying that his military friends are more broadly minded than the civilians he knows. Regardless of whether we can agree to this assertion, the law is being violated, the board is not acceptable to the people who suffer from its decisions, and the due process of law which the constitution guarantees is absent.

Since voluntary change cannot be secured, the matter has been taken into the courts. A young conscientious objector, Arthur Brandon, received a favorable decision from the hearing officer, which was reversed by the appeal board, apparently on the religious question. The state Director of Selective Service, thinking that the appeal board had acted erroneously, immediately appealed to the President. Result, affirmance without opinion. Here was a clear case where an appeal board acted arbitrarily, yet the military presidential appeal board affirmed and gave no reason. The young man being willing to submit to induction for the purpose of making a test case, was sent to Camp Upton, whence he was brought before Judge Inch in Brooklyn federal court on a writ of habeas corpus. At the trial the entire Selective Service file was placed in evidence, including the favorable opinion of the hearing officer. Since the appeal board made no memorandum of the reasons for its reversal of the hearing officer, the chairman of the appeal board was questioned with regard thereto. He indicated that the board took a narrower view of the religious test than the hearing officer did, and disagreed with him on the facts, although admitting that only the hearing officer's statement of the facts was available to the board. The F. B. I. report and the minutes of the hearing were not in the file, and were not considered.

Then the defendant placed in evidence an affidavit by General Hershey, in lieu of requiring his personal appearance, describing the procedure on presidential appeals.

General Hershey gave no indication why he differed

with the hearing officer, but merely stated that he found no reason to disturb the decision of the appeal board.

The Judge ruled that in a habeas corpus proceeding he should not review the draft classification so long as a fair hearing was had. He made no comment on the presidential appeal, finding no impropriety therein.

The case is being appealed to the United States Circuit Court of Appeals in New York.

5.

Court Procedure

IF A CONSCIENTIOUS OBJECTOR fails to establish his right to exemption before the draft boards, his next resort is the courts. He may have failed because his sincerity was not established, or because he was deemed sincere but not within the class defined by Congress as exempt. In either case he may under certain limited conditions obtain in the courts judicial review of the action of the draft boards.

Most conscientious objectors are unwilling to submit to induction, involving entrance into the army and the risk of court martial and possible death sentence if army orders are not obeyed. Prior to induction the courts have ruled in most cases that no judicial review will be allowed, on the ground that the draft board's order of induction has been disobeyed and the registrant has therefore not completed the administrative process. These cases are referred to in the chapter on judicial review. The Supreme Court of the United States now has before it a case which may settle once and for all the question whether any judicial review is open to those who will not submit to induction.* Pending the decision in that case, it is advisable for a conscientious objector, even if he cannot submit to induction, to contest in the courts the validity of his classification, al-

* *United States* v. *Falbo,* —— United States Reports ——; 87 L. Ed. 1362.

though in most districts review will be denied unless and until the Supreme Court reverses the present trend of the courts on this question.

The only sure way at present of obtaining judicial review is to submit to induction. Then by writ of habeas corpus the courts will consider whether the classification was proper. Judge Yankwich in California has allowed review by habeas corpus before induction, but this is believed to be improper, as habeas corpus tests only the validity of the process by which the prisoner is held, and prior to induction he is either not in custody, or is held under an indictment, which is in itself valid.

Although the law states that the decisions of the draft boards are final, the courts will review the classification in three instances: when there has been (1) a denial of a fair hearing, (2) an error of law, or (3) an arbitrary, capricious or unreasonable finding of fact.* The registrant must show not only that an error has occurred, but that one of these three elements is present.

In most cases the question is solely one of law; it is even a question of law whether the decision of the draft boards on a factual point was arbitrary, capricious or unreasonable.† Therefore, there is no need for a jury trial, and it is probably desirable to waive a jury. The fact of failure to report for induction, and if induction was submitted to, the validity of the induction order on its face, is not in dispute. It is therefore possible to concede the case of the government, which may be done

---

* *Angelus* v. *Sullivan,* 246 Federal Reporter 54 (C.C.A. 2nd Cir. 1917).

† *United States ex rel. Phillips* v. *Downer,* 135 Federal Reporter, 2nd Series, 521.

by entering into a stipulation of facts. In this way the trial becomes a very quick and simple matter, and thereby the defendant may avoid the longer sentence which is usually imposed on one who puts the government to the expense of a trial instead of pleading guilty.

For an instance of a conscientious objector who successfully appealed to the courts after losing his case before the draft boards reference is made to the case of Randolph Phillips discussed in Chapter 7.

When there is doubt cast by the draft boards on the registrant's sincerity, or when he clearly does not come within the legal definition of a conscientious objector as, for instance, if he is opposed only to certain wars but not to all wars or has political or economic but not religious opposition, there is no hope of success in the courts, and the defendant should plead guilty, unless he is unwilling to admit the moral implications of that word. In such cases a conviction is inevitable, as the courts will not substitute their judgment for that of the draft boards on these questions.

No matter what course is decided upon, it is desirable for the registrant to write a letter to his draft board stating that he cannot, as a conscientious objector, appear for induction if that be so, and that he will on the induction date surrender himself to the United States Attorney for prosecution. Such a letter will avoid the unpleasantness of police officers being sent to ascertain why the registrant did not appear for induction. A prompt visit to the United States Attorney will not only demonstrate that the registrant is not a draft evader, but may also induce the authorities to release him on his own recognizance or in custody of his attorney. This is frequently permitted, and when bail is required it is seldom more than $500 or $1,000.

The United States Attorney will usually take a statement from the registrant to be used in obtaining an indictment. He will then be taken before a United States Commissioner and arraigned upon a sworn complaint that he failed to appear for induction. He may have an attorney present, and may ask to be released in custody of the attorney. If bail is required, a surety company bond is preferable to an individual bond, since if a fine should be imposed, the individual surety's money may be used to pay the fine, it being presumed that this is the money of the defendant. This seems odd, but it is the law.

After arraignment the matter is presented to the Grand Jury, which hands down an indictment. The Grand Jury may ask the accused to appear before it, but seldom does so. Likewise the accused may ask permission to appear before the Grand Jury, but there is little to be gained by this, as indictment will invariably follow.

After the indictment, the case is set for pleading. The defendant must plead guilty or not guilty. If he stands mute, the court will enter a plea of not guilty for him. In some districts a plea of *nolo contendere* may be entered, meaning literally, "I do not contest," although in many districts such a plea will not be accepted. This plea, if allowed, is tantamount to a plea of guilty, but avoids the ugly connotations of that term.

At the time of pleading the defendant may, instead of

entering a plea, file a demurrer to the indictment charging that it is insufficient in some respect. By this means constitutional questions are properly raised. If a demurrer is filed, an argument on the legal sufficiency of the indictment follows before there is any trial. If the demurrer is not sustained, the defendant will then have to plead. Constitutional questions may also be raised by pleading guilty and making a motion "in arrest of judgment" immediately before the sentence is imposed.

If the plea is guilty, a probation report will usually be ordered, to enable the judge to know the character and background of the defendant before imposing sentence. If the plea is not guilty, a trial will follow, which will be before a jury unless a jury is waived.

The defendant has a right to counsel and if he cannot afford counsel, the court will assign an attorney to represent him without charge.

An appeal may be taken to a United States Circuit Court of Appeals within five days of the imposition of sentence. It is possible for the defendant to remain at liberty for a few days even after sentence for the purpose of arranging his affairs, by asking the court at the time of sentencing to fix a date for surrender.

Within thirty days after the notice of appeal is filed the record on appeal and brief must be filed, unless an extension of time is obtained. The cost of printing the record and brief is a heavy expense, but may be eliminated by permission of the court if the appellant lacks the necessary funds; he may then use typewritten papers. The expense of stenographic minutes of the trial, however, cannot be so eliminated under present practice.

The court stenographer must be paid at high rates or the minutes cannot be obtained, although the government gets a free copy of the minutes after the appellant has paid for them. Such an arrangement is manifestly unfair to poor litigants, and often denies them the benefit of an appeal.* And in rural districts it is even worse, as there is frequently no court stenographer, so that the appellant must employ one at his own expense if he expects to appeal. The Committee on Legal Aid Work of the American Bar Association has recently proposed legislation to meet this situation by establishing a reporter system under which a government employee would transcribe all proceedings and would furnish copies to poor litigants without charge, to others at fixed prices.† For the present, however, the conscientious objector who cannot pay stenographic charges is prevented from effectively prosecuting an appeal.

If the appeal is unsuccessful, a petition may be filed with the Supreme Court asking it to review by writ of certiorari. This may be granted or denied in the discretion of the court. If granted, briefs are then filed and argument had. The only case of a conscientious objector yet to reach the Supreme Court is United States v. Whitney Bowles, which went off on a side issue.‡ Other cases are on their way to the Supreme Court.

---

* Circuit Judge Learned Hand of New York has expressed doubt whether government contracts with private stenographers on these terms are not void as against public policy

† New York Law Journal, August 18, 1943, page 937.

‡ —— United States Reports ——; 87 L. Ed. 919.

6.

Judicial Review of Draft Boards

WHEN IT BECAME apparent that draft boards were making a great number of errors in classifying conscientious objectors, and that no substantial relief could be obtained from Selective Service headquarters, resort was had to the courts. Under our system of government, the courts are the last bulwark of liberty and the ultimate repository of constitutional safeguards. The independence and freedom of the judiciary are largely responsible for the freedom from oppression which the citizen enjoys. It is to the courts, then, that we turn when our rights are infringed and other redress fails. This right of judicial review is most precious, for without it we cannot secure the benefits of the civil liberties guaranteed by the Constitution. As the right of judicial review is limited and denied, so is freedom limited and denied.

It is therefore of the greatest importance in preserving the civil liberties of conscientious objectors that they should have free access to the courts to correct injustice at the hands of the administrative authorities. Unfortunately for them, and for the principles of freedom, the courts like Pontius Pilate have been unwilling to concern themselves with manifest injuries done to conscientious objectors.

The draft law contains a clause, as did its predecessor

of 1917, that the decisions of the draft boards are final.* The law does not mean quite what it says, for the courts will review decisions of draft boards in certain cases, and do not construe the draft law as depriving them of all jurisdiction.† It is well settled, as indicated in the preceding chapter, that the courts will review decisions of draft boards, despite the finality given them by the statute, when (1) a full and fair hearing has been denied, (2) a decision is arbitrary, capricious and unreasonable on the facts, or (3) a decision is contrary to law.‡ In these three instances only will the courts review what was done by the boards, and then they will not consider the case afresh, but will merely review the record of the proceedings before the draft boards.

Only occasionally does it happen that the draft boards deny a proper hearing, or act contrary to law, so that most cases where judicial review is sought fall into the remaining category, that is they involve only factual questions. In order to induce a court to review an alleged error of fact, it is necessary to show, not only that an error occurred, but further that the evidence before the board could not reasonably be said to support the conclusions reached; in other words it must be shown that the conclusions were arbitrary, capricious and unreasonable.

It is not an easy matter to upset a draft board's ruling when it must be proved to be wholly unsupported by the evidence. Nevertheless this is the law, derived from

---

* Sec. 10 (a) 2, Selective Training and Service Act of 1940.
† *Angelus* v. *Sullivan*, 246 Federal Reporter 54.
‡ *United States* v. *Kinkead*, 248 Federal Reporter 141, Affd. 250 Federal Reporter 692.

the expediencies of administrative procedure. Large areas of law are left nowadays to administrative boards for determination in order to free the courts from an unbearable burden of fact finding work. This is a necessary concomitant of the growing complexity of our economic and social structure. The courts have retained, however, some degree of control over the judicial activities which have been taken from them and given to administrative boards. Court control is exercised under the formula stated above by reviewing administrative decisions when error plainly occurred. Some students of jurisprudence see in the growth of administrative boards a grave danger for our system of government, as the citizen finds himself at the mercy of bureaucratic boards with very little recourse to the courts. Like most systems it works well when in good hands and badly in bad hands. Too often have conscientious objectors found themselves in bad hands, without recourse to the courts to correct mistakes of the boards. Here are the seeds of totalitarianism.

Far more serious, however, than the limitations on judicial review arising from principles of administrative law, is the attitude which courts have recently taken toward conscientious objectors as a result of which they are denied any review whatever.

There is a rule of administrative law that orders of an administrative agency may not be challenged by one who has flouted the agency by disobeying such orders. This is a rule of convenience, since the orderly functioning of an administrative board might be seriously disrupted if persons appearing before it could at all stages of the proceeding challenge the legality of its orders. The inconvenience caused to such persons by being unable to challenge the board's rulings in court until the proceeding is terminated is usually small compared to the inconvenience which the board and other litigants would suffer if proceedings could be broken into by the courts at any point. There is therefore, good reason for the rule, as it promotes orderly procedure, but it is merely a rule of procedural convenience which should yield whenever it thwarts rather than promotes the ends of justice.

This rule has been applied to conscientious objectors. The courts have held that a conscientious objector who fails to report for induction cannot in a resulting criminal prosecution challenge the validity of his classification, as that would be permitting attack on the draft board's order before the administrative process is completed and while the conscientious objector is violating the order.* The courts have pointed out that review of the illegal draft classification might be had by submitting to induction and seeking a writ of habeas corpus. But there are few conscientious objectors who would be willing to submit to induction for this or any other purpose, as entry into the army would violate their principles and would expose them to the rigors of court martial.

The rule announced in the foregoing decisions is a rule of administrative convenience which is applied in order to prevent the disruption of administrative pro-

---

* *United States* v. *Grieme*, 128 Federal Reporter, 2nd Series, 811; *United States* v. *Bowles*, 131 Federal Reporter, 2nd Series, 818; *United States* v. *Kauten*, 133 Federal Reporter, 2nd Series, 703.

ceedings which would result from attack upon administrative orders prior to the completion of the proceedings. Being a rule of convenience the rule should be applied only where the ends of justice are served and not where the administrative convenience promoted by the rule is out of all proportion to the hardships which will result to individuals.

Under the circumstances it is difficult to see how administrative convenience is promoted by applying the rule which was applied in these cases. The order of induction is the last order issued by a draft board and terminates its proceedings. From this point on the Army takes over, as the draft board has fully completed the administrative process so far as the Selective Service System is concerned. Judicial review after the notice of induction has been issued cannot disrupt the administrative machinery of the Selective Service System since that machinery has completed its work and no longer is in motion. Furthermore, the orderly induction of men into the Army will not be affected since no great number of individuals will be willing to face criminal charges for the sake of presenting to the courts alleged errors by the draft boards.

To be contrasted with the foregoing is the terrible burden which is placed upon a registrant if judicial review is not allowed prior to induction. He must submit to induction into the Army where he will find himself, being a conscientious objector, unable to comply with the military commands given to him. For such violations it is provided by the Articles of War* that he "shall

---

* Title 10, U. S. Code, Sec. 1536 (Article 64 of the Articles of War).

suffer death or such other punishment as a court martial may direct." If the registrant is unsuccessful in the habeas corpus proceeding, therefore, he faces death or unlimited imprisonment at the end of the court martial, not to mention the onerous treatment which may be expected by a conscientious objector at a military encampment.

It is therefore apparent that the rule announced in these cases is not necessary to the proper and orderly administration of the Selective Service System, whereas, on the other hand the conscientious objector is exposed to great hardship and the risk of extreme punishment if he accepts the only method of judicial review which is open to him under that rule.

There are cases in other circuits indicating disagreement with this rule.*

A further reason for judicial review before induction is that if all judicial review is denied to a conscientious objector who is unable to submit to induction this leaves him powerless to contest illegal action by the draft boards, and results in the administrative branch of the government having the sole power to construe and apply the laws of Congress which are given it to enforce. This would appear to be unconstitutional, both because the separation of executive and judicial powers would be absent, and because there would be a denial to the conscientious objector of his liberty without due process of law.

---

* *Baxley* v. *United States,* 134 Federal Reporter, 2nd Series, 998 (C.C.A. 4th Circuit); *Goff* v. *United States,* 135 Federal Reporter, 2nd Series, 610 (C.C.A. 4th Circuit); *Rase* v. *United States,* 129 Federal Reporter, 2nd Series, 204 (C.C.A. 6th Circuit); *Johnson* v. *United States,* 126 Federal Reporter, 2nd Series, 242 (C.C.A. 8th Circuit).

Because of their far reaching effects, these decisions were not allowed to stand uncontested. In the case of Whitney Bowles, above referred to, application was made to the Supreme Court for review, and was granted. But when the case reached the Supreme Court the government printed in its brief a ruling on a presidential appeal which superseded the plainly illegal ruling of the appeal board. Despite the fact that the government at the trial had refused to disclose the contents of this ruling or to let Bowles see his file, the Supreme Court took notice of the presidential appeal and refused to decide the main issue presented—whether Bowles' defense could be interposed although he had refused induction.* It is regrettable that the court failed to decide the issue, which however it conceded to be of public importance. Justice Jackson dissented, in a vigorous opinion with which Justice Reed concurred, in which he said:

"The court does not consider whether one may be convicted for disobeying an invalid order; and I do not care to express a final opinion on the subject, since the disposition of the matter by the court precludes its determination of the question. But I would not readily assume that, whatever may be the other consequences of refusal to report for induction, courts must convict and punish one for disobedience of an unlawful order by whomsoever made."

Because of the Bowles decision, the question is still undecided in the Supreme Court. A test case is now before the court which will settle the issue, it is hoped, before the end of the year 1943. Meanwhile conscien-

* *United States* v. *Bowles,* —— United States Reports ——; 87 L. Ed. 919.

tious objectors must enter prison without benefit of the trial by jury, the day in court, which is the inalienable right of the lowliest citizen under Anglo-American law.

7.

A C.O. Wins His Case in Court

ONE OF THE FEW conscientious objectors to win the right to exemption from a court after being denied exemption by the draft boards is Randolph Godfrey Phillips. His story is not only a lively tale, but illustrates the treatment which a conscientious objector may expect from the Army and from the courts.

Phillips is a man of high education and culture. He was Editor of the Columbia Spectator while at college, and afterward achieved some distinction as a writer on financial subjects. In the New York gubernatorial campaign of 1938, he advised Thomas E. Dewey on financial and economic problems. It so happened that at the time his induction to the Army came up he was engaged in a bitter proxy fight seeking to oust the Morgan dominated management of a tottering utility, the United Corporation. Persons unknown sought to blacken Phillips' character, and his troubles with the draft presented a perfect opportunity. But that is another story.

After he was indicted for not appearing for induction, Phillips consulted with counsel, and decided that he should report for induction for the sole purpose of testing his case in court. The court before which he would come had already ruled that no challenge to the validity of classification could be made before induction, and this had been upheld on appeal.* So it was neces-

---

* *United States* v. *Kauten*, 133 Federal Reporter, 2nd Series, 703.

sary for him to submit to induction, and risk court martial, in order to get judicial review.

The United States Attorney courteously agreed to this procedure, and consented to the dismissal of the indictment. Phillips thereupon was inducted. He was accompanied to the induction station at Grand Central Palace, New York, by a detective, who arranged to have him rushed through the ceremony, instead of waiting around for five hours as is usual. When it came to the point of the oath, Phillips of course refused. Anticipating such difficulty, he had been taken before a high officer, who did not try to force the oath upon him but merely read it to him. He then became a member of the armed forces, as the Articles of War provide that taking of the oath is not necessary; if the oath is refused, induction follows anyway.*

After the usual furlough Phillips appeared at the railroad station where he told the lieutenant at the gate that he would not willingly entrain for camp, but would do so only under compulsion. Offering no resistance, he was then escorted to a training camp by two M.P.'s. Upon arrival at camp, Phillips was not given a number and assigned to a tent like the other men, but was held apart. After being made the butt of caustic remarks by various soldiery, he was taken in hand by a sergeant who ordered him to strip for the usual examination for venereal disease. This was the first order he had received, and he politely refused to obey, on the ground that he was a conscientious objector, had been illegally inducted, and therefore could not obey any orders what-

---

* *Billings* v. *Truesdell*, 135 Federal Reporter, 2nd Series, 505.

ever. Thus he committed the deadly sin, truly deadly because punishable by death before a firing squad, of disobeying an order from his superior officer in violation of the 64th Article of War.* The sergeant then threatened to use force to compel Phillips to comply, but did not carry out his threat in the face of the cool and unflinching opposition which Phillips displayed.

The matter now went before other officers, who threatened dire consequences, until an elderly lieutenant came over to see what the row was about, and asked Phillips in kindly tone "What is the trouble, son?"

When Phillips repeated his story, cool and courteous as always, the lieutenant told him that there was no alternative but to imprison him in the guard house, where he was promptly taken. This had disadvantages, for the prisoner was conscientiously unable to participate in the drill and work which make up the daily life of an occupant of the guard house. He did consent, however, to do work which would benefit the other prisoners but not the Army, and was then detailed to clean the bunk room and latrine. He had reading material and writing paper with him to occupy the rest of the time. Incidentally, he got the best food in the camp, because the cooks were sympathetic with the prisoners and gave them the best of everything.

After a few days of this, Phillips was taken from the guard house and efforts were made to get him to take up military duties. When these failed he was told that he would be assigned to the company of a Lieutenant C, regardless. But Lieutenant C had something to say

---

* Title 10 United States Code, Sec. 1536.

about that, for when he learned that Phillips would not obey any orders, and gave good reasons for his refusal, the lieutenant refused to accept him. This left matters in the lap of the commandant of the post. After trying to bulldoze Phillips into submission and finding that this man could not be persuaded, the commandant was told by Phillips of his conscientious objection and the fact that he was at camp only as a means of bringing his case into court. Phillips complained, with irreproachable logic, that it was unfair to punish him for refusing to obey orders until there had been a final judicial determination of the legality of the induction. Until then, it could not be assumed that Phillips was legally obligated to obey orders and he should not, therefore, be punished for asserting what he claimed were his legal rights. Phillips also held forth on the error which had been committed in refusing him a IV-E classification as a conscientious objector. The good commandant had apparently never heard that there was an exemption in the draft law for conscientious objectors, and was considerably taken aback. The upshot of the interview was that Phillips was returned to the guard house.

Soon afterward, the officer who had charge of preparing a court martial case against Phillips again tried to have him assigned to duty, for the original violation on which he was held was technically faulty, and another violation must be secured in order to have him convicted. But Lieutenant C was adamant, and refused to his superior officer's face to take Phillips into his company. Finally the matter was solved, to the dis-

comfiture of the court martial officer, by Lieutenant C
agreeing to take Phillips on the understanding that he
would not be given any orders whatever. The lieutenant had defended conscientious objectors before courts
martial, and had a healthy respect for their stubbornness
and courage. So he gave orders to his sergeant that
Phillips be assigned to a tent and that he be not dis-
turbed or any orders given him by anyone. After all
this fuss and feathers, Phillips now found himself free
to roam at will within the camp limits, bound only by
the gentleman's agreement which the lieutenant had ex-
tracted from him that he not leave the post, as he was
still under technical arrest. Soon thereafter he was confined to the psychiatric ward of the hospital for "observation" although under no mental delusion except his
unwillingness to serve in the Army. Later he was placed
in the surgical ward under *de facto* arrest. The purpose of this confinement, he was told, was to prevent him
from "undermining the morale" of the troops. So matters rested until after the trial.

No less interesting than his treatment in the Army was
the treatment which Phillips received in court. He had
the misfortune to come before Federal Judge Matthew
T. Abruzzo in Brooklyn, who had earlier exhibited his
wrath against conscientious objectors when he fixed the
bail of Julius Eichel at the unprecedented sum of
$25,000.* (The case against Eichel was ultimately
dropped by the government.) Judge Abruzzo not only
made scornful remarks about Phillips' patriotism and
courage, but also took him to another part of the court-

* See New York World-Telegram, August 18, 1942; November 16, 1942.

house where a group of four hundred new citizens were about to be sworn in, and after administering the oath of allegiance, said:

"There is a person in the rear of the room whom I want to hear what I am going to say. You new citizens have taken an oath which obligates you to defend this country with your lives. There is a man in the rear who is willing to let you do this for him though he was born in this country and you were not. If you violate your oath to defend the country, the government may cancel your citizenship, but it may not revoke the citizenship of a person born here who refuses to carry out his obligations in that regard."*

The Judge not only ignored the recognition given to conscientious objectors by the draft law, but he also went out of his way to hold Phillips up to scorn before a large crowd of people. His conduct was sharply rebuked by the appellate court in these terms:

"When this petition came before the district court, the court required the draftee to take the witness stand, and examined him at length and with considerable heat. The testimony elicited did not change the picture and, in any event, should not be considered; draft boards can hardly function if evidence can be held in reserve for a trial de novo in the courts. At least no greater review can be had than that allowed for administrative agencies generally. We are constrained especially to deplore the proceeding here, as it led to the sacrifice of judicial impartiality and dignity for emotion which, however justifiable under other circumstances, had no place in the courtroom.†

Needless to say, the hearing resulted in Judge Abruzzo's summarily directing that Phillips be returned

---

* New York Times, March 19, 1943.
† *United States ex. rel. Phillips* v. *Downer,* 135 Federal Reporter, 2nd Series, 521 at pages 525-526.

to the army camp, not even making any comment on the argument offered to show that his draft classification was erroneous.

The case was immediately appealed to the United States Circuit Court of Appeals for the Second Circuit, sitting in New York City. Phillips based his main argument on the contention that Lamar Hardy, who acted as hearing officer and rejected his claim to conscientious objection, erroneously construed the law with respect to the religious requirement, and made arbitrary and false conclusions of fact which were not warranted by the evidence before him. In both respects the Circuit Court agreed with Phillips' contentions and sustained his claim, directing that he be freed from the Army because he should have been classified by the draft board as a conscientious objector.* The court's opinion, written by Judge Clark, stated:

"The facts before the draft authorities directly present this question, which is whether the draftee—in the statutory language—'by reason of religious training and belief, is conscientiously opposed to participation in war in any form,' and hence is entitled to exemption from combatant training and service. The draftee is a college graduate who has studied music, worked as a newspaper reporter on New York papers, and held some governmental and industrial positions commanding substantial wages. He resigned from his last employment in September, 1941, to devote his entire time to writing. He received his early religious training in the Presbyterian Church, although he stated that he was not now a member of any religious sect or organization. He is opposed to killing men, or assisting

* *United States ex rel. Phillips* v. *Downer,* 135 Federal Reporter, 2nd Series, 521.

directly or indirectly in the killing of men, and refused a commission in the Navy in December, 1941, because of his objection to participating in the war effort in any way. He would not fight even to repel invasion, but believes that 'war is ethically and invariably wrong.'

"He has remembered various teachings of the Christian church, such as the Lord's Prayer, the Ten Commandments, and the Sermon on the Mount, but has also read the works of 'many of the philosophers, historians and poets from Plato to Shaw.' He says that many of these men have touched his imagination and have provided him with as much religious training as a communicant of a formal church receives. 'But from whom I derived my opposition to killing men—which I judge to be the objective of combatant military service—I cannot specifically say. Yet the fact remains that I have this opposition.' The report of the Federal Bureau of Investigation which was before the Hearing Officer commented upon his character favorably; and he was described 'as a quiet, studious, reserved young man, who does a great deal of serious reading.' His references were interviewed, and apparently had no doubt of his sincerity and his long continued objection to war. In fact the reality of his belief does not seem to be in issue here. Had it been, he states that he was prepared to introduce further evidence, and that his brother, a lieutenant in the Navy now in service overseas, 'was particularly anxious to testify that my views had been held by me ever since I was old enough to understand such matters and that my opposition to war rested on basic ethical and humanitarian grounds, essentially religious in character.' His further sworn assertion that 'my opposition to war is deep-rooted, based not on political considerations but on a general humanitarian concept which is essentially religious in character,' appears, therefore, borne out by the record. It should be noted, further, that it is something more fundamental than a mere aesthetic abhorrence of physical combat and bloodshed.

"That there is no issue of fact as to the sincerity of the draftee's belief is also shown by the conclusion of the Hearing Officer made after quoting the F. B. I. report and referring to the other matters, including the draftee's testimony, before him. He says: 'This Hearing Officer is frank to state that this case is not without its perplexities. The registrant is undoubtedly sincere in his opposition to war, but whether his objections thereto are the result of his philosophical and humanitarian concepts which are deemed to have the essence of religious thought, or whether they more largely result from his political convictions and his dissatisfaction with our present way of life, is not quite clear.' He adds: 'The latter would seem to be indicated, however'; but he then proceeds to base this conclusion entirely upon a play, 'Hungryman's Library,' written by the draftee some time prior to our entrance into war. To the analysis of this work—from which he had earlier made several pages of quotation—he devotes the remainder of his report.

*   *   *

"Since the draftee offered the play in support of his claim for exemption, it may be considered for whatever it is worth in the premises. But its teachings are not so crystal clear that we should follow the course pursued by the draft officials of wholly rejecting the interpretation which its author, whose sincerity has not been questioned, himself places on it as an expression of his views. He asks us to consider the whole play, and not to identify any one character as a protagonist of his ideas. This would seem reasonable and appropriate. Throughout the play the horror of war and the importance of the position of the conscientious objector are stressed. The play takes place in a library of precious books and paintings given by the capitalist Hungryman for the edification of his fellow men, and it revolves around the seizure of the building and threat of its destruction by Bloodhart, the prototype of

Adolf Hitler. The Hearing Officer considered one of the characters, the poet Shepherd, to represent the author; and since in the course of the play Shepherd seizes a revolver and threatens Bloodhart for the safeguarding of the others present, including the heroine, Consuelo, the conclusion was reached that the author himself is not opposed to force under all circumstances. The author, we think with reason, challenges the fairness of identifying him, a mature man of thirty-two with settled convictions, with this immature poet of twenty-three, whose ideas are shown throughout to be far from solidified. Indeed, this incident, which has been so stressed as a demonstration of the author's ultimate reliance on force, appears only an attempt to give dramatic movement to the play; it is represented as leading to feelings of doubt and dismay on the part of the poet, who says: "Good God, what have I done? Can it be that military warfare will only be abolished by a conscientious objector taking arms and forcing his creed down the throat of the killers? What a colossal paradox! Is this the answer?'

"Perhaps the author intended here to present the perpetual intellectual dilemma of the conscientious objector, including himself. Certainly, however, it is hard to see in this instinctive action a denial of the views propounded elsewhere throughout the play. Thus, Shepherd has said earlier: 'Don't you see, Consuelo, this killing will go on forever unless every man becomes a conscientious objector, unless he is taught to be one from childhood, unless every nation becomes a nation of men refusing to kill for any idea or church or bank or government? How else are we to free ourselves from this eternal round of human slaughter?' And Mannheim, the man of science, perhaps a clearer protagonist of the author's ideas than Shepherd, says this in the last act of the play: 'Let us by law make conscientious objection to military killing not the eccentricity of the few but the carefully instilled educational policy of each nation's schools and universities.

"Further, if we consider the dramatic action of the play, it is to be noted that Shepherd's rather weak demonstration of force, leading to a question mark, is not the climax of the play or the means by which the library and its then occupants are saved from destruction by Bloodhart. Rather it is the persuasion of Consuelo, who allows Bloodhart to take up his box of T.N.T., by the dropping of which he could 'blow us all into the heavens.' But because of her influence upon him, he carries it out of the building. The thesis here would seem to be the power of reason in place of force. True, at the very conclusion of the play Bloodhart returns with the box of T.N.T. still under his arm and says: 'I cannot make up my mind. Once a man has started a thing he must finish it. What is to become of me if I do not blow myself up with this explosive?' And thus the curtain falls. Whether we are left to conclude that evil finally triumphs with Bloodhart's dropping of his precious bundle or that the good influence of Consuelo has saved all, and notwithstanding a certain incoherence in plot development, it is difficult to find anything in this which counteracts the general abhorrence of physical force and the philosophical belief in conscientious objection, so strongly shown throughout the rest of the play.

"The Hearing Officer does refer somewhat to a point here stressed by the Government, namely, that the play contains a criticism of the effects not merely of Fascism abroad, but of finance capitalism in this country, as portrayed by Hungryman himself, with some statements that a division of 'the plunder' must be had. But whatever the weight of the intended criticism, it is not linked to any definite political movement, nor is it clearly enough defined to be considered a political conclusion in itself. And even if it were, it appears but a correlative, and not the defining limitation, of the belief against war. We do not think it can properly be resorted to as overthrowing the force of the latter, or that the play as a whole can be considered any substantial evidence to support the draft classification.

"We conclude, therefore, that the draftee here was erroneously denied the benefits of the exemption he claimed. And we think this is an error of law, for it rests fundamentally on a different distinction between religious and political views than that which we stated in the *Kauten* case, decided some time after the Hearing Officer had made his report. We made it clear in that case that the courts cannot act as appellate tribunals for the draft machinery, and that the weight of evidence is a matter for the draft boards. Nevertheless it has been considered settled under both the Draft Act of 1917 and the present Act that errors of law are to be rectified by the courts. The various authorities are well collected and analyzed in *United States* v. *Grieme*, 3 Cir., 128 F. 2d 811. We think, therefore, that the writ should be sustained.

*   *   *   *   *

"The order denying the petition and quashing the writ of habeas corpus is reversed, and the case is remanded to the district court with directions to sustain the writ as prayed for."

Phillips' victory did not become final until several months later when the Department of Justice announced that the government would not appeal the case to the Supreme Court.*

---

* New York Herald-Tribune, September 17, 1943.

8.

Prison and Parole

GOVERNMENT IN THIS DAY and age is a creature of strange complexities and inconsistencies. Even within the same governmental departments policies exist which defeat each other. So it is with respect to the imprisonment of conscientious objectors. The Department of Justice in one breath insists on the imprisonment for long terms of men whom it will not admit to be conscientious, and in the next breath the same Department seeks prompt release from prison for the same men on the ground that they are conscientious.

This anomalous situation stems from the narrowness of the law which exempts only some but not all conscientious objectors. Those who cannot demonstrate religious basis for their views, those who might be willing to fight in certain causes but not in the present cause, and those who cannot accept any service even under civilians, are not exempted by the law, and are imprisoned. At the time of sentence the United States Attorney, who is a representative of the Department of Justice, although having some autonomy, invariably recommends a severe sentence, which the court usually imposes, the average being about three years. Protestations that the man is and has been found by the draft boards to be sincere, and is the victim of a narrow wording by Congress of the exemption, fall in most cases upon deaf ears. The government contends that these men must be punished, and they are severely punished despite the fine moral grounds upon which they may be acting. But once the conscientious objector enters prison it is another story.

The Bureau of Prisons, again under the Department of Justice, takes the attitude that a man who can demonstrate that he is sincere and conscientious should be paroled. Prison is not the proper place for him. Such parole is possible without waiting until one third of the sentence has expired, as is usually required, since the Selective Service Regulations contain a special provision* allowing parole at any time after conviction. The parole may be to (1) the armed services, (2) noncombatant service, (3) Civilian Public Service work alongside other conscientious objectors, or (4) any special work which is found suitable.

In practice, parole is not granted until one month's "quarantine" period of imprisonment has expired. Then the prisoner is given a sheaf of mimeographed forms on which to make application for parole. He must specify which of the four types of parole he would accept, and must select someone to be his parole advisor, as well as give much of his personal history. This application is then passed upon by the Bureau of Prisons for the Attorney General and by Selective Service headquarters. Both must concur in granting the parole. Their policy is to grant parole to those who are found by them to be sincere conscientious objectors, whether or not they come within the law, although in practice many sincere men have been unable to get parole, often be-

---

* Selective Service Regulations, paragraph 643.2.

cause they will not accept the limited types of parole service made available to them. Here we have a situation which is odd indeed. The Department of Justice first insists on long prison terms for these men because they are criminals, but immediately afterward tries to get them released because they are not criminals and the prisons are not proper places for their confinement. The picture is the more incongruous when it is remembered that the Department of Justice is charged by the draft law with examining claims of conscientious objectors and making recommendations to the appeal boards. When these recommendations are unfavorable, imprisonment normally follows. Because of its dual role, the same department after unfavorable action in many cases reverses its previous stand and seeks parole, finding that the subject is after all a genuine conscientious objector. In order to achieve practical justice, the department must swallow its pride and admit that it was wrong the first time.

Unfortunately, official pride is so stiff-necked that many a conscientious objector languishes in jail because to parole him would wound the pride of a department unwilling to admit its mistake.

An obvious solution which the Department has steadfastly opposed, would be to place these offenders on probation at the time of sentencing, so that they would not go to jail at all. Judges Jenney, Yankwich and Hollzer in California have done this, but other judges have refused to do so in the face of opposition from the United States Attorneys. If a man whose sincerity is conceded, or at least probable, could be sent from the courtroom directly to a C. P. S. camp or other place where he could perform useful work, the Department of Justice would never have to reverse itself, the parole problem would never arise. Perhaps such a solution is too forthright and clean-cut to appeal to Washington officialdom.

Even without a thorough-going solution such as suggested above, much would be gained by a little downright honesty in looking at the facts. Most of the men who are denied exemption are nevertheless sincere in their attitudes; otherwise few of them would prefer prison to the Army. Most of them do not belong in prison, although the conscience clause of the draft law, as narrowly interpreted by Selective Service, makes criminals of them. They are not, however, criminals in the usual sense of the word; theirs is a special case, and should be recognized as such. If the Attorney General would look a conscientious objector in the face and see him for what he is, then punish accordingly, much sorrow would be avoided. Why send these men to prison? They cannot be "reformed," more often they reform their jailers.* Imprisonment is not a deterrent to others, as they act on the basis of principle not in the fear of punishment. There is then no earthly reason for sending these men to prison, or for keeping them there, except the silly pride of officials who have previously denied them any grace and must therefore continue them in a state of eternal damnation.

Leaving now the peculiar injustice of the system of

---

* For example, two conscientious objectors who exposed conditions at their prison brought a departmental investigation down around the ears of the superintendent. See latter part of this chapter.

sentence and parole, we may examine how that system has operated.

Perhaps two thousand conscientious objectors have been convicted.* With the exception of a few who have recanted and entered the army, and a few in California who have been placed immediately on probation, all have received prison terms ranging from a few months to five years, the average being about three years. Some have also been fined, but not many.

Of these prisoners over half are members of the Watch Tower Bible and Tract Society, a militant sect also known as Jehovah's Witnesses, who claim to be ministers and entitled to exemption as such. Most are also conscientious objectors, but many are not recognized as objectors, and if so recognized refuse to serve in the camps provided for them, insisting on their exemption as ministers. Nearly all the Jehovah's Witnesses are still in prison for the rather dubious crime of believing strongly in their religious faith. Few have been offered parole, and most of them have been unwilling to accept the parole offered, which is usually limited to work at a camp for conscientious objectors.

They would be much better off preaching on their street corners than reluctantly in army guard houses or defiantly in prison. To send them to prison is to make a fetish of the principle of military service, and a mockery

---

* Official figures show 6116 persons convicted of Selective Service violations up to July 1, 1943 of which 2071 claimed to be conscientious objectors. Of these, 554 were Jehovah's Witnesses who refused to go to Civilian Public Service Camps, 114 others refused to work in the camps, 242 refused to register, 1032 refused induction, and 129 violated other provisions. See New York Times, August 27, 1943.

of the penal system. It is too bad that the law knows no exceptions, and in the immortal words of Mr. Bumble comes close at times to being "a ass." The country would be better served if the Jehovah's Witnesses were left in peace on the ground that they are undesirable for military service. The few who have found their way into the army have fully proved this by making of themselves an unmitigated nuisance.

Other than the Witnesses, there are about eight hundred men who have been imprisoned despite claims of conscientious objection. Probably ninety-five per cent of them are sincere; although in some cases there is doubt about sincerity. Apart from the few who may be insincere and who falsely claimed conscientious objection as a way to avoid military service, the rest fall into four classes.

The first and probably the largest class comprises those who are true conscientious objectors as defined by law, but were not sufficiently articulate or fortunate to succeed in demonstrating their right to the exemption. They are the casualties of the human frailty of their judges. Secondly, there are the political and economic objectors, who object to the purposes for which this war is fought, rather than to war as an immoral method. They are the victims of a fear on the part of Congress, wholly unwarranted by the facts, that Communists might use conscientious objection to shield themselves from military service. The third group are those who are sincere conscientious objectors but lack religious basis for their views. Many of these are religious in the broad sense of having humanitarian and moral principles upon which they order their lives, but belong to no church and subscribe to no creed or theology. This group is the victim of a narrow-mindedness on the part of Selective Service officials, and a lack of clearness in the law itself. Finally, there are a few thorough-going objectors who cannot accept the conditions of exemption, either because they will not register, or will not serve in the way provided for conscientious objectors. Many will not serve in any way under the draft. These comprise six per cent of British conscientious objectors.

Under the superior law and superior administration of it which obtains in England, all these men, allowing for human errors, would be exempted. But here they are in prison, and likely subjects for parole. No figures are available to show how many paroles have been granted, or how long a time was served before the parole came through. But the paroles have been slow in coming, usually many months, and have been granted only to a small minority. Some of the reasons for this have been suggested. Others may be only guessed at. But beneath it all is the failure to look at the problem for what it is, a problem of getting men out of prison who do not belong there and should not have been put there. If the prison officials had the only say-so in these matters, the problem might be handled in this light, but the interference of Selective Service officials, always thinking in terms of public relations, and the supervision of the Attorney General's office, always thinking in terms of crime and punishment, have made progress very slow.

There is one class of prisoners who require special mention: those who cannot be paroled because they are conscientiously opposed to working in a camp for conscientious objectors. The regulations permit parole to other forms of work; any job which is suitable in the individual case will satisfy the requirement of the regulations. But for reasons which are not known, the Director of Selective Service has persistently blocked the granting of paroles to special work, although it is reported that the Bureau of Prisons favors such parole where that suits the needs of the particular case.

Because paroles are being allowed only to enter the armed forces or a Civilian Public Service camp, those men who were imprisoned either because they insist on unconditional exemption, or object to the type of work done in the camps, have not been paroled. Protesting against the unfairness of this policy, two conscientious objectors, Stanley Murphy and Louis Taylor, undertook a hunger strike while in Danbury prison. They fasted for eighty-two days, being forcibly fed toward the end of this period to prevent death. Finally they stopped the fast when, as they thought, they had gained their objective of release either unconditionally or to work which they could accept. After tireless efforts of friends of Murphy and Taylor, the Selective Service administration finally relaxed its opposition to special paroles, and agreed to allow men to be paroled to work projects under some governmental or public agency in addition to the previous types of parole. Murphy and Taylor had gained a point for all prisoners who had not been freed on parole because they would not go to the camps. For themselves, however, they gained not the anticipated parole, but a terrible retribution from the Bureau of Prisons, the horror of which has made their case a *cause célèbre.*

Apparently in punishment for their hunger strike, Murphy and Taylor were sent to a hospital for insane prisoners at Springfield, Missouri. For a long time no one could find out what was happening to them. They were held incommunicado, even their mothers not being allowed to hear from them. Fearing for the life or the sanity of her son, Mrs. Murphy at great personal sacrifice made the trip to Springfield in the hope of being allowed to see Stanley. She finally succeeded in seeing him only to find that he had been treated so horribly that there was indeed reason to fear for his sanity. In the weakness resulting from his long fast, his mind might not stand the tortures to which he was subjected.

Although designed only for use with the violently insane, the boys were confined to "strip cells" where they were left stark naked in a stone dungeon without furniture of any kind and with a hole in the floor for a toilet.* Such confinement, alone, cold, and naked, is a form of torture which would do the Gestapo credit. As if this were not enough, they were beaten by their guards, although the guards of course denied this. Telling of the beating, Stanley Murphy wrote in a letter which was smuggled out of the prison:

"I myself have experienced the 'strip cell' and the 'monotonous diet' as I told you. I did not tell you of the beating I received on Tuesday, August 3rd. As you know I had, from the beginning, made clear the position I took

---

* New York World-Telegram, August 25, 1943; The Catholic Worker, New York, July-August, 1943; The Conscientious Objector, New York, August, 1943.

and still hold on the matter of work. It was known to the men in charge. * * * Nevertheless, on this Tuesday, two attendants opened the door of the 'strip cell' and threw in a pair of pajamas, which I put on, and they took me to the shower and told me to emery paper the shower stall. I replied that I was not able to do so. They then summoned another attendant from outside and said they would make me do it. With the arrival of the outside attendant the business started. The first blow to the jaw must have dazed me for the next thing I knew one man had both his arms around my neck and choked and dragged me along the floor, while another kept hitting me in the stomach. After a while they let up, and one said 'throw him into the cell and let him rot there.' The names of the attendants who did the beating were ———— and ————. I have given their names to Dr. King and Mr. MacCormick. * * * During this time Lou (Louis Taylor) had been removed to E-1 East and one attendant told me it was the practice there to beat the men three times a day. Later, an inmate managed to tell me that Lou had asked him to tell me that they had beaten him badly. * * * Many men have come to me simply to express their willingness to testify as to the treatment they and others here are receiving."*

Because of the frightfulness uncovered by dint of long probing behind the veil of prison censorship, the Director of the Bureau of Prisons, James V. Bennett, consented to an investigation, after the American Civil Liberties Union had taken steps to bring the whole matter before the courts in a habeas corpus proceeding. An impartial investigator, a prominent penologist of the highest reputation, Austin MacCormick was named to

----

* See New York World-Telegram, August 25, 1943; The Conscientious Objector, New York, September, 1943.

conduct the inquiry into the treatment of the conscientious objectors at Springfield. Later two others were added as investigators, Charles W. Palmer of the American Friends Service Committee and Dr. M. R. King of the United States Public Health Service.

These investigators interviewed Dr. Cox, head of the unsavory institution, and his assistants. They reported that Murphy and Taylor had in fact been confined to strip cells, and Mr. MacCormick in particular expressed the opinion that such treatment was improper.* The investigators were unable to prove the charges that the men had been beaten, but expressed no dis-belief in the statements of the two boys. It was their word against the guards' so that definite proof was probably impossible.

Mr. Bennett, the Director of Prisons, had previously declared that strip cells were used only for violently deranged patients and not as punishment. Never at any time was there any question that Murphy and Taylor were mentally deranged. They were transferred to Springfield, and confined in strip cells as admitted by Mr. Bennett, solely for disciplinary reasons. Whether one believes their story of the beatings, or believes the guards' undoubted denial, the treatment which they admittedly received is wholly unjustified in a civilized society.

A prominent physician, Dr. Evan W. Thomas, pointed out that strip cells are properly used only for the confinement of violently demented prisoners, whereas officials had admitted that Murphy and Taylor were not

* New York World-Telegram, August 25, 1943, August 27, 1943.

even psychotic cases. Dr. Thomas said that to give a prisoner such punishment "is an obvious effort to humiliate and degrade him to a sub-human level," and that, "when the Germans resorted to such measures in their concentration camps, the world was shocked."*

After receiving the report of the investigators, Mr. Bennett is reported as having refused to say whether the strip cells would be abolished or methods of treatment changed.† Abandoning hope of getting decent treatment for these men by voluntary action of the prison authorities, the American Civil Liberties Union immediately started legal action‡ by writ of habeas corpus to determine whether the men were properly confined in a mental hospital although sane, and whether their horrible treatment was not such cruel and unusual punishment as the Constitution forbids.

In addition, the Civil Liberties Union urged that conscientious objectors who would not work be sent, as in the first World War, not to prisons (where they may be beaten or at best put in solitary confinement for not working) but to prison camps where they could engage in farm work or some other labor in a guarded enclosure under their own management.§

---

* New York World-Telegram, August 27, 1943.
† Same.
‡ Same.
§ New York World-Telegram, August 31, 1943.

9.

Cat and Mouse

A CAT PLAYING with a mouse does not kill him all at once; she repeatedly attacks and releases her victim, thereby prolonging his discomfiture and her enjoyment. A similar process was applied in England to conscientious objectors in the first World War, whereby they were repeatedly prosecuted, imprisoned, released and prosecuted again for virtually the same offense. This was known as the cat and mouse treatment.

The law contains a safeguard against repeated punishment for a single offense; it is one of the cardinal principles built into the common law of England to protect the rights of man against the overweening power of the state. This principle was a part of the law which the colonists brought to our shores, and found its way into our Bill of Rights, which says:

"Nor shall any person be subject for the same offence to be twice put in jeopardy of life or limb."*

The familiar rule stated above prevents the cat and mouse treatment being used in most cases, but it does not prevent a second prosecution for an offense which differs in any respect from the first. The second prosecution may be for the violation of the very same provision of the law but still there is no double jeopardy if the second violation is another offense. This happens, for

---

* United States Constitution, Amendment 5.

instance, when a man refuses to register for the draft. He is imprisoned. Upon release from prison he again refuses to register. The same law is violated but a separate offense has occurred because of the separate act of refusal. So it happens that when the law imposes a continuing duty to perform an act, refusal to perform is a continuing and repeated offense which may be made the subject of successive prosecutions and imprisonment. This can last as long as the duty remains and is refused.

It is apparent therefore, that when a positive act is required by law, the duty so to act may survive after a period of imprisonment for refusal to perform the act. If so, a second violation occurs and there is no double jeopardy within the meaning of the Constitution because there is a separate offense.

When the die-hard pacifists, or absolutists, who refused to comply even with the symbols of conscription by registering, were prosecuted, it was feared that they would be given the cat and mouse treatment when they emerged from prison. Although the law allows this, good morals do not, and the Attorney General was therefore asked to give assurance that he would not allow it. It is said that he did give such assurance in general terms.

Matching the year which conscripts were first required to serve, the first non-registrants received one-year sentences. But soon we entered the war, and the soldier was required to serve for the duration of the war, so it did not seem fair to let a draft violator off with a one-year sentence. The sentences were gradually stepped up until the average is now three years, the maximum still standing at five years by statute. When the first men had completed their terms and left prison, their fellows were still facing long terms in the army or in C. P. S. camps. It was therefore natural for prosecuting officials to want to keep the objectors confined for similar terms.

For this reason cat and mouse prosecutions are being brought. Although he has not felt that he could prevent them altogether, the Attorney General has notified all United States Attorneys that they may not start such a prosecution without his consent. Some control is therefore exercised to prevent undue harshness in repeated prosecutions. It is difficult to see why, however, a man who has once paid the penalty should continue to be jailed for a continuance of his refusal to obey. The fact that the judges are now handing out stiffer sentences than he got the first time is certainly a poor reason. There is something to be said for treating these men the same as others, but it is doubtful whether comparisons may be properly drawn between prison sentence and service in a C. P. S. camp or the army.

Here again, the desire to maintain good public relations is probably the cause of governmental strictures on the conscientious objector. A single critical letter to a public official from the wife or mother of a soldier, embittered at her loss and angry that a "conchie" should be let out of prison while her boy is risking his life, may in wartime produce more immediate and far-reaching results than a heritage of tolerance and freedom centuries old.

10.

Constitutional Questions

NOT LONG AFTER the Selective Training and Service Act became law, its constitutionality was challenged. Five young men who had refused to register, acting on conscientious scruples against participation in war by any compliance with a conscription law, were indicted in New York City, and filed demurrers challenging the constitutionality of the law.*

Since many of the constitutional objections to the law are reflected in the attitudes of conscientious objectors toward conscription, there is point to discussing these questions, although since Pearl Harbor they have become academic, as the Supreme Court held in 1918 that conscription is valid in time of actual war.† Furthermore, there are rumblings of thunder on the horizon which foretell a stormy future for conscription legislation which will doubtless be offered after the war in an effort to put the United States on a permanent military basis like that which prevails in many European countries. If this happens, the points raised here will again become important.

The constitutionality of the Selective Training and Service Act was challenged in the following respects:

The safeguards of the Bill of Rights are obliterated,

---

* New York Herald Tribune, December 4, 1940. See also Philadelphia Record, December 12, 1940.
† Selective Draft Law cases, 245 United States Reports 366.

including the fundamental rights of freedom of speech, freedom of the press, freedom of petition and assembly, the right to trial by jury, and the right to the writ of habeas corpus. It is clear that any power of Congress, in peace time, to conscript citizens if valid is superior to all the great rights guaranteed to them by the first ten amendments of the Constitution, and the exercise of that power necessarily makes citizens no longer free, but slaves of the military machine. Since the guaranties of the Bill of Rights are absolute, indeed the cornerstone of democratic government, they cannot be swept into the discard by implication. The power of Congress to supersede the Bill of Rights must clearly appear within the four corners of the Constitution itself. Whatever Congress may do in time of war which will limit the operation of the Bill of Rights, it does not appear anywhere in the Constitution that the Bill of Rights may be set at naught in peace time.

A second attack on the draft law has reference to the sort of notice and hearing provided in classifying registrants. These are plainly inadequate, and as to conscientious objectors at least, the failure of the statute to embody the proper constitutional safeguards of adequate notice and fair hearing was not only unconstitutional, but undemocratic and unwise, since much of the injustice meted out to conscientious objectors can be traced directly to this source. The haphazard postcard notice provided by the act fails to meet proper standards and has had a part in many minor tragedies. Too often has the time to appeal slipped by or the time to file papers expired unkown to the registrant because of delay in his receiving a postcard. Fortunately the authorities have usually been lenient in this matter, but nevertheless the notice is inadequate. Registered mail would have avoided all difficulty by furnishing proof of receipt.

More important by far is the failure to provide for fair hearings. Nearly all of the rights so carefully protected in courts of law are denied to a draft registrant, including the right to have counsel, the right to public trial, to be confronted by the evidence, to have witnesses, commonly summed up as the right to a day in court. By contrast the British law grants all these rights and others, so that hearings before the British tribunals are similar to trials at law, while our hearings, on the other hand, more resemble the Inquisition. Because of the inadequate regulations, draft hearings, as might have been expected, do not have the flavor of impartial fairness which is the pride of Anglo-American justice, but smack of the bureaucratic and high-handed procedures which are the curse, and may one day be the downfall, of the Roosevelt administration as of countless autocracies before it. The only possible excuse for such methods is the exigency of war, and even this excuse was lacking when the draft law was enacted. A return to constitutional procedure would do much to make any post-war conscription more palatable, and, what is more, would remove a serious fracture in the fabric of our Constitution.

In addition to the failure to provide for proper hearing, there is the failure to provide for judicial review. If the courts cannot correct the errors of draft boards, then the governing influence of the judiciary is removed, and draft procedures become well-nigh lawless. This is especially sinister because the Act also contains an invalid delegation of power to the executive. Through delegation of power, and lack of judicial control, the delicate balance between legislative, executive and judicial power is upset. By placing in his hands the power both to construe and to apply the law, as well as the power by writing regulations to legislate, the Director of Selective Service is made in very truth a dictator within the field laid out for him by Congress. This fact has been sharply brought to public attention by Congress having found it necessary several times to consider legislation to nullify regulations adopted by the Selective Service authorities. Government by decree is bad enough under any circumstances; when in addition all review by the courts is removed, then it cannot even be called government, it is despotism. Reference to the Constitution should hardly be necessary to demonstrate the invalidity of such procedure. Elsewhere in these pages its unwisdom is shown. As before, the Constitution has shown itself to be sound, and short cuts unsound. The shortest way to the desired end is often the longest way around.

The most serious of these attacks is as follows: that the power to raise and support armies does not include the power in peacetime to conscript armies, the right of conscription being limited to the militia, which may be compelled to serve the Federal government only to suppress insurrection or repel invasion, actual or imminent. If this is so, conscription is constitutional only in time of war or immediate threat of war, and the decision* of the

---

* Selective Draft Law Cases, 245 United States Reports 366.

Supreme Court in the first World War that wartime conscription is constitutional does not control the validity of the present law.

The force of this argument appears from a mere reading of the Constitution, which provides in Article I, Section 8, that "the Congress shall have power * * * to raise and support armies," and "to provide and maintain a navy" but limits the compulsion of military service by granting Congress power only "to provide for calling forth the militia to execute the laws of the Union, suppress insurrections, and repel invasions."

Historically, the militia was the only force which could be conscripted and has always comprised all able-bodied men of military age. When, therefore, the Constitution limits the use of the militia to wartime exigencies, it limits the use of conscription to wartime.

Since Pearl Harbor these questions have become academic. As a matter of historical interest, however, it is important to note that the power of Congress to conscript was probably intended by the founding fathers to be limited to the use of the militia in case of invasion and insurrection, but did not permit the conscription of armies in peacetime. The power "to raise and support armies" was intended to confer only the power to raise armies in the manner usual to the times, namely by voluntary enlistment.

This view finds support not only in English and American legal history, but also in political history. Peacetime conscription was never attempted until the World War. The Civil War draft was bitterly opposed and never fully enforced. Once before a draft had been attempted, in the War of 1812, but was abandoned after Daniel Webster made a furious speech against it. This speech shows that the power of conscription was universally regarded as limited to the uses of the militia specified in the Constitution. Webster said, in part:

"This bill indeed is less undisguised in its object, and less direct in its means, than some of the measures proposed. It is an attempt to exercise the power of forcing the free men of this country into the ranks of an army, for the general purposes of war, under color of military service. To this end it commences with a classification which is no way connected with the general organization of the militia, nor, to my apprehension, included within any of the powers which Congress possesses over them. All the authority which this Government has over the militia, until actually called into its service, is to enact laws for their organization and discipline. This power it has exercised. It now possesses the further power of calling into its service any portion of the militia of the States, in the particular exigencies for which the Constitution provides, and of governing them during the continuance of such service. Here its authority ceases.

       *   *   *

"But, sir, there is another consideration. The services of the men to be raised under this act are not limited to those cases in which alone the Government is entitled to the aid of the militia of the States. These cases are particularly stated in the Constitution, 'to repel invasion, suppress insurrection, or execute the laws.' But this bill has no limitation in this respect. The usual mode of legislating on the subject is abandoned. The only section which would have confined the service of the militia proposed to be raised, within the United States has been stricken out; * * *

"This, sir, is a bill for calling out the militia, not according to its existing organization, but by draft from new created classes;—not merely for the purpose of 'repelling invasion, suppressing insurrection, or executing the laws,' but for the general objects of war—for defending ourselves, or invading others, as may be thought expedient; —not for a sudden emergency, or for a short time, but for long stated periods; for two years, if the proposition of the Senate should finally prevail; for one year, if the amendment of the House should be adopted. What is this, sir, but raising a standing army out of the militia by draft, and to be recruited by draft, in like manner, as often as occasion may require?

*　　*　　*

"The administration asserts the right to fill the ranks of the regular army by compulsion. It contends that it may now take one out of every twenty-five men, and any part, or the whole of the rest, whenever its occasions require. Persons thus taken by force, and put into an army, may be compelled to serve there during the war, or for life. They may be put on any service, at home or abroad, for defense or for invasion, according to the will and pleasure of the Government. This power does not grow out of any invasion of the country, or even out of a state of war. It belongs to government at all times, in peace as well as in war, and it is to be exercised under all circumstances, according to its mere discretion. This, sir, is the amount of the principle contended for by the Secretary of War.

"Is this, sir, consistent with the character of a free government? Is this civil liberty? Is this the real character of our Constitution? No, sir, indeed it is not. The Constitution is libelled, foully libelled. The people of this country have not established for themselves such a fabric of despotism. They have not purchased at a vast expense of their own treasure and their own blood a Magna Charta to be slaves.

*　　*　　*

"Congress having, by the Constitution, a power to raise armies, the Secretary contends that no restraint is to be imposed on the exercise of this power, except such as is expressly stated in the written letter of the instrument. In other words, that Congress may execute its powers, by any means it chooses, unless such means are particularly prohibited. But the general nature and object of the Constitution impose as rigid a restriction on the means of exercising power as could be done by the most explicit injunction. It is the first principle applicable to such a case, that no construction shall be admitted which impairs the general nature and character of the instrument.

"A free constitution of government is to be construed upon free principles, and every branch of its provisions is to receive such an interpretation as is full of its general spirit. No means are to be taken by implication which would strike us absurdly if expressed. And what would have been more absurd than for this constitution to have said that to secure the great blessings of liberty it gave to government an uncontrolled power of military conscription? Yet such is the absurdity which it is made to exhibit, under the commentary of the Secretary of War.

"But it is said that it might happen that an army could not be raised by voluntary enlistment, in which case the power to raise armies would be granted in vain, unless they might be raised by compulsion. If this reasoning could prove anything, it would equally show, that whenever the legitimate power of the Constitution should be so badly administered as to cease to answer the great ends intended by them, such new powers may be assumed or usurped, as any existing administration may deem expedient.

*   *   *

"If the Secretary of War has proved the right of Congress to enact a law enforcing a draft of men out of the militia into the regular army, he will at any time be able to prove, quite as clearly, that Congress has power to create a Dictator.

*   *   *

"Sir, in granting Congress the power to raise armies, the people have granted all the means which are ordinary and usual, and which are consistent with the liberties and security of the people themselves, and they have granted no others. To talk about the unlimited power of the Government over the means to execute its authority, is to hold a language which is true only in regard to despotism.

*   *   *

"Those who cry out that the Union is in danger are themselves the authors of that danger. They put its existence to hazard by measures of violence, which it is not capable of enduring. They talk of dangerous designs against Government, when they are overthrowing the fabric from its foundations. They alone, sir, are friends to the union of the States, who endeavor to maintain the principles of civil liberty in the country, and to preserve the spirit in which the Union was framed."*

The change in public opinion which can be wrought by the passage of time is strikingly illustrated by the contrast between this speech and the lack of public outcry at the first peacetime conscription in our history under the Burke-Wadsworth Bill.

Although most carefully briefed and fully argued, both the trial court and the Circuit Court of Appeals failed to discuss the issues raised, and readily found the law to be constitutional,† resting their decisions on the theory that the power to raise armies is not limited to wartime, and ignoring altogether both the significance of

---

* Writings and Speeches of Daniel Webster, Vol. XIV, pages 55-69.

† *United States* v. *Rappeport*, 36 Federal Supplement 915 at pp. 916. 917; *United States* v. *Herling*, 120 Federal Reporter, 2nd Series, 236.

the militia clause of the Constitution and the fact that this power conflicting with the Bill of Rights must be weighed against it. The trial judge reasoned thus:

"The Constitution in some of the provisions expressly refers to 'time of peace' and 'time of war,' Art. 1, Sec. 10, Amends. III, V. See Art. 1, Sec. 9. The provisions of the Constitution granting power to Congress to raise and support armies, and to provide and maintain a navy and to make rules for the government and regulation of the land and naval forces, however, do not restrict the exercise of such power to 'time of war' nor do they impose any limitation as to the time or manner of exercising such power. It can not be assumed that the Constitution intended to prevent the raising of an army by voluntary enlistment or conscription until war has been declared or actually begun. The provisions can not be construed so as to restrict the exercise of the power in a way requiring a delay that may render the grant of the power useless.

"Even if Congress has not the power to conscript in time of peace, or if some of the provisions of the Act are unconstitutional, the indictments may not be dismissed.

"The indictments charge the defendants only with failure to register.

"It is well established that Congress has the power to secure needed information relative to legislative action through registration and answers to questionnaires."

No appeal was taken to the Supreme Court because of the exhaustion of funds and the fear that the Supreme Court also would dodge the issues raised.

The author of the Selective Training and Service Act, Grenville Clark, New York lawyer, has now drafted the Austin-Wadsworth Bill, which would impose total mobilization of all manpower.*

---

* S. 666; H.R. 1742, 78th Congress, 1st Session.

The next step, which has had the blessing of high officials in Washington, is the permanent conscription in peacetime of all young men and women as they reach military age. We would adopt the institutions of Hitler in our fear of him. It would be a cruel mockery if such a law were to be foisted on the American public in the hysteria of wartime. Their good sense would never permit its adoption when we are at peace. Even Mrs. Roosevelt, staunch friend of youth and youth organizations, has publicly proposed that all young people be drafted for a year of service to the state before leaving college. There is no question that all such proposals violate every fiber of our Bill of Rights, and are not only unconstitutional, but destructive of the entire philosophy which underlies our Constitution. If the day comes when such proposals are sanctioned by the American people, they will have abandoned their Constitution.

11.

Involuntary Servitude

ANOTHER CONSTITUTIONAL question which has often been raised relates to the Thirteenth Amendment which prohibits involuntary servitude. The confinement of conscientious objectors to labor camps where they are forced to work without compensation appears, at first blush, to be involuntary servitude. Nevertheless it is clear that such work, authough involuntary, would not be held by the courts to be a violation of the Thirteenth Amendment.

Certain types of service to the state, although uncompensated and compulsory, have been held by the courts not to be slavery or involuntary servitude, as prohibited by the Constitution. For instance, a Florida statute requiring able-bodied males between twenty-one and forty-five years of age to work six days a year on the public roads unless they could hire a substitute was held constitutional by the Supreme Court of the United States, in an opinion which states:

"Utilizing the language of the Ordinance of 1787, the Thirteenth Amendment declares that neither slavery nor involuntary servitude shall exist. This amendment was adopted with reference to conditions existing since the foundation of our Government, and the term involuntary servitude was intended to cover those forms of compulsory labor akin to African slavery which in practical operation would tend to produce like undesirable results. It introduced no novel doctrine with respect of services always treated as exceptional, and certainly was not intended to interdict enforcement of those duties which individuals owe to the State, such as services in the army, militia, on the jury, etc. The great purpose in view was liberty under the protection of effective government, not the destruction of the latter by depriving it of essential powers."*

As indicated, the state has long assumed the power to compel its citizens to serve, involuntarily, on juries and in the militia. It was not so long ago that colonial towns saw all able-bodied men between eighteen and forty-five drilling on the green once a week. This service was compulsory, and necessary to preserve the state from attack. But the right of the state to compel such service was never in question. In the same way the state was wont to require many other forms of service from the citizen, who discharged his duties to the sovereign with the sweat of his brow while building public works or performing other needed tasks. With the specialization of labor which has now developed, the need for calling on the citizen to render service in physical ways has almost disappeared. The citizen now pays taxes instead, although he still must serve physically on rare occasions as by jury duty and service in the militia. The fact that such incidents of citizenship have largely fallen into disuse now that the citizen can discharge his duties more conveniently through taxation does not alter the principle that the state may compel physical service.

It thus appears that the involuntary servitude prohibited by the Thirteenth Amendment extends only to service to a private master, and does not limit the right

---

* *Butler v. Perry*, 240 United States Reports 328.

of the sovereign to compel physical service in the categories mentioned above.

Every able-bodied male citizen of military age, by laws which are centuries old, owes a duty of military service to the state, which need not compensate him therefor. This is called militia service. If the state gives him the privilege of performing an alternative service, as Congress has done with respect to conscientious objectors, the essential character of the service may be said to remain unchanged; it is a service to the nation in time of peril, which is part of the duty of every male citizen of military age.

However unfair may be the discrimination between army pay and the total lack of compensation, even maintenance, for conscientious objectors, this does not affect the constitutional question. Discrimination in itself is not unlawful, and here the test of legality is not the compensation paid, but the involuntary character of the service. A slave may be well compensated but remains a slave, while a free man may work for nothing yet still be free.

The courts have rejected the argument that the draft law imposes involuntary servitude on conscientious objectors in violation of the Thirteenth Amendment.* On the other hand it may be argued that the power to compel military service does not include the power to compel one who is exempted from military service to serve in a civilian capacity. If the civilian labor were clearly related to the national emergency, there would be little doubt that such labor could be compelled. But many

---

* *United States* v. *Mroz*, 136 Federal Reporter, 2nd Series, 221.

of the present projects for conscientious objectors have little or no relation to the emergency and may therefore be regarded as improper and illegal substitutes for military service.

While it is difficult to express an opinion on the principles involved, novel and abstruse as they are, it can be safely predicted that the courts will not invalidate any reasonable service required in wartime of conscientious objectors in place of military service. And even in theory, I doubt whether the Thirteenth Amendment limits the ways in which the state may require the citizen to discharge the obligations of citizenship. If the service required of conscientious objectors is unconstitutional, it is not because it is slavery, but because civil rights are destroyed.

Service to the state is not slavery; it is citizenship. The state may compel proper citizenship, although when compulsory it is but a pale reflection of the real thing. If, however, the state should find it necessary to compel the citizen in peacetime to render service to the state, civilian or military, the Constitution need not be invoked; it would have been abandoned.

12.

Refusal to Register

ONE OF THE first defects of the draft law to become apparent was the failure to provide a separate register for conscientious objectors as was done in England. There are a small minority of pacifists who call themselves absolutists. They believe that any compliance with conscription is wrong, even though it be merely the act of registering for military service. They would have been willing to register as conscientious objectors, but this the Act did not permit; they were required to register with all other conscripts, and they refused to label themselves conscripts by registering.

Prosecution was, of course, inevitable. In fact some of the absolutists welcomed it, as they were anxious to bear witness in a dramatic way against conscription. Most, however, were indifferent, and neither flinched from prison nor did they welcome it.

To many, the refusal to register appears to be a quibble. All that the registrant is asked to do is to identify himself and submit to a sort of census for the purpose of determining who is eligible for military service. Exemptions for conscience can be claimed and will be determined in due course. Most of the information called for by the registration card was given voluntarily by those who refused to register, when they wrote letters to the prosecuting or draft officials giving the desired information. Since they gave their names and adddresses in such letters, it seems indeed a quibble for them to refuse to put the same data on a registration card. But to men of the absolutist stamp even the symbol of compliance is important. They deny the right of the government to make them sign anything under a law designed to raise armies. They follow a higher law.

A further reason was given by some for refusing to register. The law does not provide complete exemption for those who oppose any service whatever. For them there would be little point to registering, as they could not hope to gain the exemption which their conscience requires.

The first to be prosecuted for refusal to register were eight students at Union Theological Seminary. All of them pleaded guilty, refused to ask for leniency, and were sentenced in New York federal court to terms of a year and a day.* Ironically, they would all have been exempted from any form of service had they registered, as they were divinity students. Also ironically, they were automatically registered later at the prison under the draft regulations. Why could not the government have registered these men, once they identified themselves, and avoided this prosecution since they would later be registered at prison?

Not long afterward, the refusal of five other young men to register afforded an opportunity to test the constitutionality of the draft law. Unlike the divinity students, these men did not plead guilty but filed demurrers attacking the constitutionality of a peacetime draft.

---

* New York Times, November 15, 1940, page 1.

After losing their case they too were sentenced to imprisonment for terms of eighteen months and two years.* The penalty grew more severe as the war grew older.

One of these men, Stanley Rappeport, did not abandon the fight when the constitutional point was lost, but attempted to convince a jury that they should acquit him because he acted in obedience to a law higher than that which the judge told them required a conviction. Rappeport tried his own case without a lawyer. He succeeded in making quite a speech to the jury, but they quickly found him guilty. After all, they were not judging him by his law, but by theirs.

Although most of the non-registrants were anxious to bear witness for their pacifism, they did not achieve much success, for the public could not easily understand why a man who would be exempted if he registered and asserted his claim should refuse to do so. From courtroom observation of the reactions they obtained, it is my opinion that the non-registrants mostly failed to impress others, but were regarded as young and foolish, or as crackpots. The example which they may have set for other pacifists is quite another matter.

The final chapter in the government's treatment of non-registrants concerns those over the military age of forty-five years. A group of about twenty men over forty-five, who were required to register but exempt from military service, refused to register on conscientious grounds. All of them wrote letters to the Attorney General or to Selective Service officials explaining the reasons for their action. The reasons were not capricious or

---

* New York Times, February 12, 14 and 15, 1941.

immature, as these men had mostly been conscientious objectors in the first World War, and knew whereof they spoke when they refused to participate in conscription.

Although younger non-registrants had been prosecuted and sentenced up to five years in prison, the Department of Justice chose to take a different attitude toward this older group. They were not prosecuted, the letters which they wrote being regarded as sufficient identification of themselves, and practical compliance with the registration requirement. This was a sensible attitude for the government to take; the more is the pity it was not taken sooner.

One, however, of this group was prosecuted. After being imprisoned and held in high bail, he was finally released when the Attorney General was induced to drop the prosecution. This man was Julius Eichel; his case is discussed in the next chapter.

13.

The Eichel Case

THE CASE OF Julius Eichel is worthy of comment because of the furor which it caused and the extraordinary circumstances involved. Julius Eichel is a chemist, a quiet-spoken man, living with his wife and son in Brooklyn. Being over forty-five, he is not liable for military service but was nevertheless required to register with others in his age group. Eichel refused to register, along with several others who were also over forty-five.

During the first World War, Julius Eichel was one of those who suffered physical torture for their conscientious objection. Through suffering they eventually obtained release to a prison camp where they had considerably more freedom than in prison. But in the process Eichel became convinced that conscription was an evil with which he could never compromise.

So it was that when his age group was called upon to register, Julius Eichel refused to comply, writing instead a letter to the Director of Selective Service explaining why he could not register. The other men did likewise. Since many of these were prominent men engaged in work of vital importance to the national welfare, the government was reluctant to prosecute them, especially since they had profound convictions and wide influence, the sort who would be sure to cause a great stir if they were made to suffer martyrdom. After all, they were not being registered for military service, but only for a possible draft of manpower, and their crime was therefore not too serious. One of the men was a doctor, engaged in important research. Faced with the loss of a key man, the U. S. Public Health Service intervened with the authorities. It was accordingly decided by the Attorney General that none of the men who wrote letters to the authorities explaining their stand would be prosecuted. Instructions to this effect went out to the United States Attorneys for the various districts.

Despite this arrangement, perhaps through some departmental misunderstanding, Eichel's arrest was caused by the office of the United States Attorney in Brooklyn, New York. Also for reasons which are not known, Eichel was indicted and the prosecution against him proceeded although the other men were not being prosecuted.

A hue and cry was immediately raised by Eichel's fellow "criminals," demanding that they too be prosecuted. But overtures made to the prosecutor and the Attorney General were without avail. Accordingly, prominent friends of Eichel went to see the Attorney General, and pointed out the injustice of prosecuting only one of the group and not the rest. Still nothing was done.

Meanwhile Eichel was arraigned in federal court in Brooklyn, and released on bail of $2,500. After indictment, he appeared on August 18, 1942, for pleading and stood mute, unwilling to admit or deny the charge. The court thereupon entered a plea of "Not Guilty," and without any request having been made by the prosecution, raised the bail to the unprecedented sum of $25,000. Judge Matthew T. Abruzzo, who took this extraordinary action, indicated his reason therefor by saying to the defendant, "I'll make sure you don't get out until you are tried, if you want to act that way about it."*

Eichel had done nothing to arouse the antagonism of the judge; in fact he had stood silent except to state that he would remain mute rather than plead.

Regardless of how he may have disapproved of Eichel's views, the judge should not have fixed bail at $25,000 unless that was necessary to ensure his appearance. Such sums are reserved for murderers or notorious criminals, who may attempt to flee the jurisdiction of the court. Eichel, however, had appeared voluntarily whenever requested and had given the court every reason to believe that he would be available when wanted for trial. Under these circumstances, bail would normally have been nominal. In most such cases, no bail at all is required. In any event, high bail cannot properly be used for purposes of punishment, or to confine to jail a defendant of whom the judge disapproves.

The United States Attorney afterward interceded with the judge for a reduction in bail. Thereupon the judge agreed to reduce the bail to $5,000, although even this sum was very high under the circumstances, and beyond the defendant's means.

In addition to the unusual action regarding bail, Judge Abruzzo disposed of the motion of Eichel's counsel to dismiss the indictment on the ground that the Selective Service Regulations provide that men in this age group who refuse to register shall be registered by the United States Attorney signing the registration card for

---

* New York World-Telegram, August 18, 1942.

them. The regulation was drafted, as Eichel's counsel pointed out, for the specific purpose of preventing prosecutions such as that before the court. "In the entire United States," the judge was told, "this man alone was singled out for prosecution, although this regulation applied to all the others and they were all registered under it."* Judge Abruzzo summarily denied the motion before Eichel's counsel had finished his argument, and without hearing any rebuttal from the prosecutor.

After several postponements the case came on for trial. It so happened that Judge Abruzzo was again presiding in criminal cases, and would therefore try the case. Knowing this, Eichel's counsel asked the Attorney General to arrange a postponement until the following month when a different judge would be sitting. This was apparently the desire also of the government, as the prosecutor when the case was called asked for an adjournment until the first day of the next month's term of court. The judge refused to consider it. Eichel's counsel then spoke up to say that he thought the Attorney General wanted the adjournment. "I don't care what the Attorney General wants," Judge Abruzzo replied.† Nevertheless, after a whispered conference with the prosecutor, the judge consented to the adjournment. But before doing so, he again threw a bombshell into the courtroom by raising the bail once more to $25,000, again saying that he wanted to put Eichel "right in jail where he belongs."‡ The judge's action is subject to the interpreta-

---

* New York World-Telegram, August 18, 1942.
† New York World-Telegram, November 16, 1942.
‡ Same.

tion that he not only used bail for punishment, but also pre-judged the case in assuming that Eichel was guilty and belonged in jail. Eichel's counsel announced his intention of seeking a writ of habeas corpus to reduce the bail, which could be appealed to a higher court,* but before this was done anonymous persons came forward with $25,000 in cash, and Eichel went free.

To cap this amazing tale with an anti-climax, when the case again came up for trial before another judge, the government entered a *nolle prosequi*, thereby abandoning the prosecution.

---

* New York World-Telegram, November 16, 1942.

14.

Military Control of Camps

THE DRAFT LAW requires that conscientious objectors "be assigned to work of national importance under civilian direction."* This requirement has not been scrupulously respected, as the over-all control and direction of the camps in which conscientious objectors are confined rests in the hands of the Camp Operations Division of Selective Service Headquarters, which consists almost entirely of army officers, wearing uniform. Here, as in the case of presidential appeals, the spirit if not the letter of the Selective Training and Service Act has been violated by the Director of Selective Service appointing army men to positions which should have gone to civilians. Perhaps this is the natural result of appointing an army man to head Selective Service. But the Director of Selective Service is an administrator, not merely a soldier, and should be able to find civilians to work with him. There can be no doubt that Congress intended that conscientious objectors be placed entirely under civilian control. By putting army officers in charge at the top, the whole program comes under military domination in violation of Congress' plain intention.

While there can be no doubt that the spirit of the law is violated, there is some question as to the letter. Most conscientious objectors are sent to camps set up by the

---

* Sec. 5 g, Selective Training and Service Act of 1940.

National Service Board for Religious Objectors, created by pacifist churches, which acts as the agent of the government in providing facilities for conscientious objectors and has general responsibility for the operation of the camps under the Camp Operations Division of Selective Service. The army men who comprise the Camp Operations Division issue orders relating to the camps, which are transmitted by the National Service Board to the camp directors. The latter are in immediate charge of operating the camps in all respects except the work itself, which is under the supervision of a technical civilian agency of the government.

Thus the immediate control both of work and other phases of camp life remain in civilian hands, and the agency having general administrative responsibility is also civilian. But at the top of the structure, controlling all, are the army officers of Camp Operations Division and General Hershey himself.

If the army officers confined themselves to general supervision and the laying down of broad policy, they would probably stay within the letter of the law, as they might be said not to be exercising direction of the work. But if they issue orders affecting particular issues or intervene in the details of camp operation, then they surely exercise such control of the work as to amount to illegal direction.

It is difficult to ascertain whether army men have interfered in the immediate direction of the work. It is known that they have issued orders relating to hours of work and furloughs, and have even specified punishment in cases of infraction of discipline. It appears as though a fairly close degree of supervision exists, so that the army men are truly running the camps. Certainly that is the attitude which the army men themselves have adopted; Colonel Franklin A. McLean presented a memorandum on November 26, 1942, to the training school for Directors of C. P. S. camps stating the official policy thus:

"The impression that camps are democracies to be run by the assignees is entirely erroneous. They may suggest or recommend but only the decisions and orders of the Director will be recognized by Selective Service."

* * *

"From the time an assignee reports to camp until he is finally released he is under control of the Director of Selective Service. He ceases to be a free agent and is accountable for all of his time, in camp and out, twenty-four hours a day. His movements, actions and conduct are subject to control and regulation. He ceases to have certain rights and is granted privileges instead. These privileges can be restricted or withdrawn without his approval or consent as punishment, during emergencies or as a matter of policy. He may be told when and how to work, what to wear and where to sleep. He can be required to submit to medical examinations and treatment and to practice rules of health and sanitation. He may be moved from place to place and from job to job, even to foreign countries, for the convenience of the government regardless of his personal feelings or desires."

This whole discussion boils down to an inquiry as to the meaning of the term "direction" as used in the statute. If Congress intended that general supervision and control should be civilian then the present scheme is illegal, but if only the immediate control of the work need be civilian then there is something to be said for the legality of the army men's operation of the camps. In either case, however, only a technical and legalistic reading of the law will sustain General Hershey's management; under any fair view of the intention of Congress, he is exceeding his authority.

Such callous disregard for the wishes of Congress is hard to understand. Representations have been made to the General on this point and got nowhere. Increasing dissatisfaction with the way in which the army men were trying to run the camps on military lines has led to open revolt. Some of the campers had planned a conference at Chicago to discuss problems of interest to them, in a genuine desire to improve the situation of the conscientious objector. General Hershey, not wanting the conference to be held, took steps to prevent it by issuing an ordder cancelling all furloughs until further notice. Many of the men had been saving up furlough time so that they could go to the conference. Most of them went A.W.O.L. to attend, although this meant loss of all furloughs for many months to come. The conference was held, and in dignified and democratic discussion produced fruitful results. One would think that General Hershey would have welcomed such a conference and would benefit from it, but even if he thought it harmful, to interfere as he did certainly is to assume immediate direction of the life of conscientious objectors—the sort of direction which Congress sought to place in civilian hands.

Because military control over the camps could not be removed by other means, resort has been had to the courts. Charles Butcher of the school at Cheltenham,

Maryland, for delinquent colored boys, staffed partly by conscientious objectors, was dismissed because he protested too vigorously the whipping of pupils. He was then assigned to another project, to which he refused to go on the ground, among others, that the work projects were illegally directed by military men. Indictment followed, and a trial in federal court at Baltimore at which the defense showed in great detail the extent to which military men controlled the camps. Butcher was convicted, but on advice of counsel took no appeal because the order which he violated, being merely to report to a work project, might be upheld, although an order relating to the work itself could be attacked as invalid.

Another case which squarely raised this issue was brought before the federal court at Buffalo, the case of Max Kampelman from the camp at Big Flats, New York. He sued out a writ of habeas corpus while working at the camp to test the validity of his being held there under military control. Thus he was not guilty of any infraction, as was Butcher, and the court must pass on the merits of his contention. This case, as yet undecided, has the support of the National Committee on Conscientious Objectors.

Altogether, the administration of the camps is fairly good. Such instances of dictatorial control as the banning of the Chicago conference are to be deplored, but on the whole the camps are well run and democratic procedures are allowed. What is particularly objected to both by the campers and their friends outside is the assumption of Selective Service headquarters as reflected by Colonel McLean that the conscientious objectors in the camps are subject to their absolute control, just as men in the army. The men in the camps are profound individualists, and like to stick to democratic ways of doing things, by which means they have succeeded in creating a fine atmosphere for living and working under the most difficult circumstances. When army officers step in and start imposing military discipline, they object, and rightly so.

15.

Why C.O.'s. Are Not Paid

ONE OF THE complaints most often heard about the work program for conscientious objectors is that they are unpaid. Indeed, they and their churches pay for their maintenance. When the program was first drawn up this question was discussed, and Clarence Dykstra, then Director of Selective Service, said that he did not think an appropriation could be obtained from Congress for work camps under private auspices. The three religious bodies, Quakers, Mennonites and Brethren, then agreed to try to finance it themselves. This was a large undertaking. The program costs well over a million dollars a year. Without cost, the government gets the labor of some six thousand able-bodied and mostly willing young men, who turn out about ten times as much work as an equivalent number of C. C. C. men used to do. The conscientious objectors, their families and churches in general accepted as inevitable the necessity of paying for the maintenance of the men. But before long a new problem arose.

With the shortage of labor becoming more acute, men were taken out of the camps and put on farms or in hospitals, where their work was vitally needed. This made it possible for their maintenance to be provided, also made it possible for them to receive wages. In fact, many of them must be paid so that other employers and workers would not complain of free labor being supplied to their competitors. But here a snag was struck. The official who holds the government's purse strings is the Comptroller General. He ruled that the conscientious objectors could not be paid under a plan where they proposed to donate their wages to support of the camps for other conscientious objectors. This plan was devised to prevent inequality between paid workers outside the camps, and unpaid workers in the camps.

The reasoning of the Comptroller General apparently is that conscientious objectors are a species of slave to the government and anything which they earn belongs to the United States Treasury. He reaches this strange result by examining the law and finding nothing which authorizes the men to keep their pay. He fails to state that he also found nothing to prevent it. Here is the gist of his opinion:

"No provision of law which would warrant the use of the funds for the purpose proposed in your letter has been cited by you and I am not aware of any such provision."*

That is all there is to it. The proposal is disapproved because no law permits it, although it is hard to conceive why a law must be passed before a farmer can pay his farm-hand wages.

The opinion does not make very good sense. Nevertheless it must stand, as, in order to keep politics out of government spending, the Comptroller General has been made accountable only to himself and to God, and unless Congress shall circumvent his decision by changing the law, it cannot be upset.

---

* Letter from Comptroller General to General Hershey dated December 8, 1942, numbered B-27231.

Later on another proposal was made to the Comptroller General, that the Coast and Geodetic Survey employ conscientious objectors, and pay their maintenance and $5.00 per month wages out of funds which were available for the purpose. The Comptroller General disapproved the payment of any wages because, he said, it was not shown that it was necessary to pay the men any wages, even pocket money, in order to secure their services. This opinion borders on the ridiculous, as who could expect men to do good work if they are prevented from having even a few pennies to spend on small conveniences? It should be noted also that both the Director of Selective Service and the Secretary of the Treasury had urged the Comptroller General to permit the desired expenditures.

There appears to be little hope of correcting this situation. Although the rulings may be unjustifiable in law, no means presents itself of getting a court to upset them. For there is no contract between a conscientious objector and his employer which could be made the basis of a suit. He is assigned to work by the government, and has no contractual rights at all. Therefore he has nothing which he can enforce in a court of law.

As men with dependents begin to be drafted, the problem of pay becomes acute. Families of service men receive generous allowances from the government, but families of conscientious objectors will go to the poor house.

The dependency complication, however, suggests a way in which to test the validity of the Comptroller General's ruling. While the conscientious objector himself has no basis for suit, nor has his dependent wife, because they have no contract on which to sue, the divorced wife of a conscientious objector might ask the divorce court for a judgment against him to pay alimony. Such a judgment might be enforced against the wages earned by the divorced husband and frozen by the Treasury in a special fund.

If some such means should arise of getting the question before the courts, it is believed that the Comptroller General's rulings will be declared erroneous, and the way will then be opened for conscientious objectors to work on a much larger scale at jobs which provide maintenance.

Unaffected by the Comptroller General's rulings is the right of C. P. S. men to receive wages, as the rulings prohibit only the use of wages for certain public purposes. If General Hershey could be induced to allow the men to receive wages and keep them, much hardship for the men, their churches, and dependents would be avoided. Congress has appropriated money for this purpose, but General Hershey thinks it is "good public relations" for the men to go unpaid, and unpaid they remain.

A comparison of these difficulties with the British method of assignments to useful and paying jobs, discussed in Chapter 17, makes it pitifully plain that we are far behind them in common sense as well as justice.

16.

The Right to Public Office

FOR MANY YEARS pacifists have been respected members
of the community, and have been freely admitted to
places of public trust, as lawyers, teachers, judges and
political office holders. But occasionally there has been
question raised as to the qualification for public office of
one who will not bear arms to defend his country.

An applicant for admission to the Bar of the State of
Illinois, Clyde W. Summers, was denied the right to practice law solely because he is a conscientious objector. As
in most states, an aspirant to the legal profession in
Illinois must pass an examination into his character as
well as his ability. The character examination is conducted by a committee of lawyers and judges who consider the applicant's moral fitness to practice law. This
committee determined that Summers was not qualified
to practice law in Illinois because he is a conscientious
objector, although he was well qualified in all other
respects. Apparently the committee felt that the oath
required of a lawyer that he support and defend the
Constitution could not be subscribed by a pacifist, and
in any event that a pacifist lacks the good moral character
required of a lawyer. Summers is taking the matter
before the courts.

The same question arose in New York, but there the
character committee had no difficulty in finding the

applicant qualified to practice law although a conscientious objector. In fact, there are cases on record in New York where the authorities have made special dispensations to permit conscientious objectors to be admitted to practice when the time was short before they were to go to camp.

There is only one question involved here, and that is whether a conscientious objector is a man of good character, who can properly exercise the public trust reposed in a lawyer. To this question there can be but one answer: conscientious objectors are not only men of good character, but demonstrate their willingness to make personal and economic sacrifices as well as to suffer criticism for the sake of moral principles. Such men are unusually well endowed with the moral strength which is needed in a lawyer. The opposite conclusion could only be reached by ignoring the sincerity of a conscientious objector, and treating him like the draft evader or "slacker."

History lends support to the proposition that conscientious objectors are qualified to practice law. Not only have many pacifists been lawyers, some of them prominent, but pacifists generally have enjoyed public confidence for their honesty and moral character. The best known of pacifist groups, the Quakers, have a reputation for honesty, and have held many positions of public trust, especially in Pennsylvania.

Another office which has been denied to a conscientious objector is that of teacher in the public schools. In July, 1943, the Assistant Attorney General of the State of Kentucky ruled that a conscientious objector could not lawfully be reappointed as a teacher after having been in a camp for conscientious objectors, under a State law that teachers could be discharged only for "immorality, misconduct in office, incompetency or wilfull neglect of duty." The ruling held that a conscientious objector is *ipso facto* guilty of all these offenses, and went on to state:

"The fact that the individual in question has served a term in a concentration camp set aside for persons such as he indicates that at least he has been guilty of an offense involving moral turpitude, and that his conduct has been such that an orderly society must remove him from circulation."

From this quotation it is obvious that the official did not have any conception of the status of a conscientious objector under the law. He does not serve a term for an offense against society any more than the man in military service. Such a ruling cannot be taken seriously, but the fact that such rulings can be made is serious, and calls for protest not only by pacifists, but by all who are interested in civil liberties.

As in the case of a prospective lawyer, there can be no question that a school teacher who is a conscientious objector may be of good moral character despite his attitude toward war. But in the case of a teacher something more is involved, for the teacher is in a position to indoctrinate young people with his philosophy. Therefore it may properly be required of a teacher that he do not teach doctrines which are objectionable to the public, or at least that he present all sides of controversial questions. If, then, a conscientious objector were engaged in teaching his pupils to oppose military service, he might properly be denied the right to teach, although it is not so clear that a teacher could not properly present both sides of the case for and against war, or of pacifism and militarism. But the teacher is not usually called upon to teach such things, and surely he is no worse at teaching mathematics or language because he happens to be a pacifist.

Employment in government jobs of a clerical nature has at times been denied to conscientious objectors in addition to more responsible positions of public trust. A bill was even introduced in Congress* to deny employment in federal jobs to persons claiming to be conscientious objectors.

With regard to political office, the same question recurs. No case comes to mind, however, of a candidate for political office being disqualified because of his refusal to take up arms. Quakers and other pacifists have from time to time held political office without any such question being raised. It has been questioned, however, whether a conscientious objector can properly take the oath required of public servants.

The Constitution requires that nearly all holders of State and Federal office "shall be bound by oath or affirmation to support this Constitution."† In carrying out the Constitutional provision, Congress has prescribed the following form of oath:

"I do solemnly swear (or affirm) that I will support and defend the Constitution of the United States against all enemies, foreign and domestic; that I will bear true faith

---

* H.R. 2142, 78th Congress, 1st Session.
† United States Constitution, Article 6.

and allegiance to the same; that I take this obligation freely, without any mental reservation or purpose of evasion. * * * "*

There can be no doubt that many pacifists have taken this oath, and without mental reservation, in the belief that they were required to support and defend the Constitution only by means other than military. Such an interpretation is a reasonable one, as the usual means of supporting and defending our laws and principles of government is by social and political methods, not by force of arms. No less an authority than Charles Evans Hughes, when Chief Justice of the United States Supreme Court, took this view. In a case involving the oath required for naturalization, he wrote in a dissenting opinion:

"It goes without saying that it was not the intention of the Congress in framing the oath to impose any religious test. When we consider the history of the struggle for religious liberty, the large number of citizens of our country, from the very beginning, who have been unwilling to sacrifice their religious convictions, and in particular, those who have been conscientiously opposed to war and who would not yield what they sincerely believed to be their allegiance to the will of God, I find it impossible to conclude that such persons are to be deemed disqualified for public office in this country because of the requirement of the oath which must be taken before they enter upon their duties. The terms of the promise 'to support and defend the Constitution of the United States against all enemies, foreign and domestic,' are not, I think, to be read as demanding any such result. There are other and most important methods of defense, even in time of war, apart from the personal bearing of arms. We have but to con-

* United States Code, Title 5, Section 16.

sider the defense given to our country in the late war, both in industry and in the field, by workers of all sorts, by engineers, nurses, doctors and chaplains, to realize that there is opportunity even at such a time for essential service in the activities of defense which do not require the overriding of such religious scruples. I think that the requirement of the oath of office should be read in the light of our regard from the beginning for freedom of conscience. While it has always been recognized that the supreme power of government may be exerted and disobedience to its commands may be punished, we know that with many of our worthy citizens it would be a most heart-searching question if they were asked whether they would promise to obey a law believed to be in conflict with religious duty. Many of their most honored exemplars in the past have been willing to suffer imprisonment or even death rather than to make such a promise. And we also know, in particular, that a promise to engage in war by bearing arms, or thus to engage in a war believed to be unjust, would be contrary to the tenets of religious groups among our citizens who are of patriotic purpose and exemplary conduct. To conclude that the general oath of office is to be interpreted as disregarding the religious scruples of these citizens and as disqualifying them for office because they could not take the oath with such an interpretation would, I believe, be generally regarded as contrary not only to the specific intent of the Congress but as repugnant to the fundamental principle of representative government."*

Despite such convincing reasoning, the Supreme Court in the case from which the above quotation is taken decided that the oath required of one seeking naturalization as a citizen could properly be interpreted as

---

* *United States* v. *Macintosh*, 283 United States Reports 605, at pp. 630-632.

requiring a promise to bear arms. We therefore have the anomaly that the oath given to citizens who take public office may be properly taken by a conscientious objector, while the same oath prevents a conscientious objector from becoming a citizen. This comes about through the insistence of the immigration officials, before giving the oath, on asking specifically whether the applicant for citizenship would be willing to bear arms in defense of his adopted country. The oath itself does not require such a promise, and as Justice Hughes stated is generally interpreted as not requiring the bearing of arms. It is to be hoped that with the wider recognition given in law to conscientious objection, the barrier which prevents them from being naturalized will be removed. This could be done simply by the immigration officials eliminating the embarrassing question, or by the Supreme Court overruling decisions holding that such a question is proper.

Despite occasional attacks on their attachment to the Constitution, and despite the exclusion of alien pacifists from the privilege of citizenship, the conscientious objector is generally recognized as a good citizen. He may be regarded as foolish or misguided in his reliance on good will instead of violence, but he is nevertheless respected, and allowed to hold positions of public trust. Whenever his attachment to the principles of our government is attacked, the conscientious objector should make it clear that he is devoted thereto, although he differs with the majority on the appropriate means for preserving the Constitution against its enemies.

17.

The British Draft Procedure, a Comparison

PERHAPS THE STRONGEST indictment of the drafting of the American law and regulations affecting conscientious objectors, as well as the administration thereof, arises from a simple comparison with the way the same job is done in Great Britain. When it is realized that for a long time before our law was written the British law had been in operation, and that studies had been published of the administrative experience in England,* the indictment of American draftsmen and administrators becomes damning. The record showing nothing to the contrary, it must be presumed that congressional committees and others who prepared the statute as well as the men who wrote the regulations neglected to give consideration to the British experience. If they had given it consideration they could hardly have failed completely to benefit from such an admirable model.

The text of the British statute of 1939 in so far as it affects conscientious objectors is printed in an appendix to this work. It applies to all male British subjects between the ages of 18 and 41 resident in Great Britain.

Instead of registering for military service as in this country, the British conscientious objector registers separately on a register for conscientious objectors. At first

---

* e.g., "The National Service Act," published July, 1940, by Central Board for Conscientious Objectors, London.

he registers provisionally, and only after proof of sincerity does he become permanently registered as a conscientious objector. Until he has had hearings before the tribunals, he cannot be put on the military register or called for military service.

Here occurs the first mistake in our draft law, as nothing was done to make provision for those who would refuse to sign a register for military service. Because of this, several score young men were imprisoned who would all have had hearings in Britain, and if sincere would have received exemption from military service.

For failure to register the British law imposes a fine of £5; our law imprisonment up to five years, a fine of $10,000, or both. If a Britisher refuses to register he is hailed into court, fined a small sum, and then, if he claims to be a conscientious objector, is registered on the provisional register of conscientious objectors. An American in the same circumstances is imprisoned from one to five years, then registered on release from prison, and if he does not fill out his questionnaire, again imprisoned for practically the same offense. These comparisons are startling, especially when it is remembered that our law, with all its harshness, was enacted when war was remote from us, while the British were already in the throes of conflict.

The next step after registration is the application to a local tribunal for classification. Instead of asking a lot of catch questions, and inquiring about church and theological matters, as does our Form 47, the British form simply calls for "any statement you wish to submit in support of your application." The applicant's statement must therefore be in his own words, without benefit of any clues as to the sort of answers desired, or any barriers in the form of trick questions, such as are contained in the American questionnaire.

The applicant may specify whether his objection is addressed to all military service or only to combatant service. If he does not have general objections to military service as such, but objects on political grounds to service in this particular war, he may indicate this by stating that he is opposed only to being included in the military register. It will be noted that the grounds for exemption are not limited. Only one requirement is imposed by the British law, the requirement that the objection be founded in conscience. All kinds of objection are recognized, so long as they are conscientious.

By comparison our law, as usually construed, would exclude all who cannot trace their objections to some teaching of a purely religious nature, the humanitarian philosophical and political objectors all being excluded from the benefit of the exemption. Even as most broadly interpreted in the *Kauten* decision, referred to elsewhere,* (which Selective Service headquarters has not accepted) the exemption of the American law does not extend to political or economic objectors, or objectors to this particular war, and covers only those who in some sense can be called religious. The narrowness of the American law in this respect has sent hundreds of upright and capable young men needlessly to prison, all because of a vague Congressional fear of Communism, and ineptitude on the part of the War Department in

* See Chapter 2.

drafting this provision of the law, coupled with a rigid interpretation of the law.

There are sixteen local tribunals for the whole of England, Scotland and Wales, each consisting of five members, of whom three comprise a quorum. Since the number of boards is few as compared to the local boards of the United States, the caliber of men chosen is much higher. Whereas the local board in the United States is usually in complete ignorance as to how to handle the problem of conscientious objection, if not openly intolerant, the British local tribunals perform this task quite satisfactorily on the whole. The appointment of British board members is better suited to obtaining good material, as they are chosen with care by the Minister of Labour and National Service with due regard for the selection of persons who are impartial in the matter of conscientious objection, and after consultation as to at least one of the appointments with trades union representatives. The chairman must be a County Judge.

The appointments to American boards, on the other hand, are made by the Governor of the State submitting a list to the President. The Governor takes recommendations from others, and if the usual procedure is followed, most of the appointments must have been arranged through political or personal connections. The gigantic task of appointing thousands of board members was undertaken in the space of a few weeks, so that the appointments could not have been considered with such care as to produce persons impartial or even qualified in the matter of conscientious objection. Again the haste with which we swung into the draft has caused us many a headache.

The Appellate Tribunal in England has four divisions, with a fifth for Scotland and a sixth for Wales. Each tribunal consists of three members, who are men of outstanding reputation and considerable legal experience, such as retired judges, administrators and civil servants. The small number of boards and centralization of work again makes for efficiency and ability as well as promoting uniformity, qualities often lacking under our procedure. The personnel are chosen in the same way as in the case of the local tribunals, and are equally satisfactory. In contrast, our appeal boards are pretty well staffed but often have not the knowledge or ability to handle conscientious objection. In some cases our appeal board members have decided appeals without even taking the trouble to read the law.

In the case of Whitney Bowles, which reached the Supreme Court,* the chairman of his board, a well-known lawyer and politician, denied him the right to exemption on the ground that he did not belong to a pacifist religious sect, although that was the test of the 1917 law, not the present law. Despite such incompetence, board members who have demonstrated their unfitness are unaccountably allowed to continue to function, although the same could hardly happen in England.

The procedure at the local tribunal is radically different in Britain. The hearing must be public; ours is private and often there is no hearing at all. The applicant may be represented by a solicitor (lawyer) or by a friend who may conduct the case on his behalf; the American procedure expressly denies the right to coun-

* See Chapter 6.

sel. The British applicant may call witnesses to testify under oath and for the record, and may produce documentary evidence; the American regulations do not prevent this, but the advantage of witnesses and documents is almost lost when the applicant is not represented by counsel, so that most of our hearings consist of questioning of the applicant by the draft board. Most generously, the British Minister of Labour will pay the expenses of the applicant himself and of his witnesses in attending the hearing, although expenses of counsel are not paid. Under our procedure, if the applicant cannot afford to go to the hearing, or to bring witnesses, he does without. There have been cases in this country where the hearing on appeal, which is the only thorough hearing held, was scheduled for a place over 100 miles away from the home of a poor applicant, and he, being desirous but unable to attend the hearing, was classified *in absentia*.

From this it can be seen that the British, having behind them centuries of struggle for the rights now guaranteed to a defendant in court, were careful to preserve these rights under the draft, whereas the American draft regulations, as shown in the chapter on procedure, give the registrant short shrift at an inquisitorial sort of hearing. As has been suggested, this may be due to the trend under the Roosevelt administration toward administrative bureaus running everything and taking short cuts through the delays involved in regular judicial procedure. We might do better here, as in other aspects of government, to make haste more slowly under the ponderous but careful methods which our fathers fought and died to establish.

In Britain the local tribunal may decide the case of a conscientious objector in one of these ways: (1) He may be classified as entitled to unconditional exemption, and not required to perform any sort of service; if so he is simply registered in the Register of Conscientious Objectors without conditon. (2) He may be registered as a conscientious objector but under the condition that he perform work of a certain general nature specified by the tribunal, which may be private or public, for wages or for maintenance only, but must be civilian in character and under civilian control. (3) The applicant's name may be removed from the Register of Conscientious Objectors, where it was originally entered provisionally, and placed on the Military Service Register for noncombatant duty. (4) The applicant may be registered on the Military Service Register for combatant duty.

The tribunal will, if conditions are imposed, specify some particular line of work which must be followed, but it is left to the individual to find suitable employment. If he is engaged in work of importance to the community, he will usually be directed to remain there; if not, he will be told what else to do. If he cannot find a proper job, he must report back to the tribunal which may at any time change the conditions to meet his requirements. In the cities, many men were assigned to "fire watch" during the period of bombing, although a large proportion remained in jobs of a purely private nature.

There are some who object even to fire watching, but as a wag pointed out, it is difficult to see how anyone but a fire worshipper can object to fire prevention as such, although it may be argued that putting out fires helps the war effort. Most conscientious objectors, however, have been willing to save human life and private property in air raids.

The most frequent conditions on which exemption is granted, other than civil defense including air raid precautions and fire watching, are landwork in farm or forest, relief or humanitarian work as in hospital or ambulance service, and lastly employment in private business, which frequently means staying on at the old job. This is not always possible, however, as a number of employers discharge conscientious objectors. Even the British Broadcasting Company has been guilty of this intolerance.

If absolute or conditional exemption is not allowed, the remaining categories call for military service. Noncombatant service, as in the United States, may include any service not requiring the employment of weapons, but usually means in Britain attachment to a Labour Corps, while in this country it is now confined to service in the Army Medical Corps.

Those conscientious objectors who cannot persuade the tribunals to grant any exemption face a £200 fine or two years imprisonment. The original penalty was £100 or one year, which was later increased. This contrasts with the penalty in our law of $10,000 fine or five years imprisonment, which was not only imposed when we were still at peace, but is exacted of many sincere conscientious objectors who are not covered by the law, as it is interpreted. We therefore send innocent men to jail for periods up to five years, whereas in Britain the attempt is made to jail only the actual draft evader, and then for a maximum of two years.

In England, however, there is no possibility of judicial review in the criminal courts, but the thoroughness of the trial before the draft tribunals perhaps obviates the necessity for judicial review. Here, where the draft boards give only the scantiest of hearings, or none at all, judicial review is sorely needed but cannot be obtained unless the Supreme Court overthrows the prevailing rule in the lower courts.*

The alternative to prison is entrance into His Majesty's armed forces, with court martial if orders are not obeyed. The procedure here is similar to ours, except that the British military trials are more public.

There is a striking difference in the procedure after court martial. Here the sentence of imprisonment, for life or less, is executed in a civil prison and cannot be terminated except by pardon or, after one-third of the time has been served, by parole. In Britain, if the court martial sentence is for three months or more, the prisoner may, if he still claims conscientious objection, apply to the appellate draft tribunal for release, regardless of the fact that he previously may have been denied exemption by the appellate tribunal. The tribunal may then order the Army to release the prisoner and may impose the usual conditions for draft exemption, just as though there had never been any interlude of army service and court martial. This is a right of great value, as the draft tribunals keep constant control of court martialled offenders and may at any time order their release. In the

---

* See discussion in Chapter 6.

United States, the draft boards lose all authority after a man has been inducted into the army, and even the courts will not review his case unless there has been a flagrant and obvious error.

This privilege applies only to one who originally claimed to be a conscientious objector, but even for the man who discovers for the first time after entering the army conscientious scruples against service therein, relief is provided in Britain in the form of an application to the appellate draft tribunal, sitting as an Advisory Tribunal, which may advise the War Office to release him as a conscientious objector.

In the United States, if a conscientious objector applies for exemption from military service after being inducted into the army, he may be released only if the military authorities wish to grant this privilege. There being no special procedure for review in such cases, the army will ordinarily grant release only if in the best interests of the service and has little regard for the well being of the individual. He might possibly obtain redress from a court but would find it difficult to establish the sincerity of his position to the extent required in habeas corpus proceedings because of his failure to make the claim before the draft boards.

There are vastly more conscientious objectors in England than in the United States, some 45,000 having been granted exemption as compared with about 6,000 granted exemption from military service in the United States and probably an equal number who have entered non-combatant service. The reason for this is apparent to anyone who is familiar with the history of pacifism in

Europe after the last war. There were at one time over a score of members of Parliament who had taken the so-called Oxford oath never to support another war. The Peace Pledge Union of men and women who pledged themselves never to participate in war numbered many thousands and was not looked upon with the intolerance and lack of understanding which similar groups experience in the United States. The membership in American pacifist organizations numbers only about 12,000 today, although this does not include many Quakers and members of other religious sects who are pacifists.

The British figures* showing results of draft board decisions as to conscientious objectors are interesting. Up to January 1, 1943, the local tribunals had granted unconditional exemption to 2,700 objectors who are required to render no service whatever, having demonstrated that they are conscientiously opposed to any service under the conscription acts. These comprise 5 per cent of the total of registered conscientious objectors. Those who have been given conditional exemption and are required to perform some sort of civilian work number over 20,000 and make up 37 per cent of the whole. Many of these work in private industry while others are engaged in civilian defense. They are assigned individually and not regimented and segregated as in the United States. Over 15,000, or 29 per cent, have been given non-combatant military service and the same proportion have been denied any exemption and ordered to

---

* The figures which follow are all taken from the lists published by the Central Board for Conscientious Objectors, London, as of January 1, 1943.

combatant duty. The appellate tribunals have made changes in a great number of cases as follows:

Of 16,264 appeals heard up to the end of the year 1942, exactly half were varied by the appellate tribunal, although in a great many cases the variation was only in the kind of work required to be performed as a condition to exemption.

The following table shows the results of these appeals.

Local tribunal classification		Appellate tribunal classification	
Complete exemption.	4	Conditional exemption.	2
		Combatant service.	2
Conditional exemption	1,585	Complete exemption...	100
		Conditional exemption (decision of local tribunal unchanged)....	669
		Conditional exemption; condition of work varied on appeal.	659
		Noncombatant service.	137
		Combatant service.	20
Noncombatant service	6,034	Complete exemption...	75
		Conditional exemption.	3,073
		Noncombatant service (decision of local tribunal affirmed).	2,783
		Combatant service.	103
Combatant service...	8,641	Complete exemption...	74
		Conditional exemption.	2,068
		Noncombatant service.	1,818
		Combatant service (decision of local tribunal affirmed)	4,681

In addition to these cases, the appellate tribunals, sitting as Advisory Tribunals, heard 383 applications for discharge from the armed forces, in which 79 were not recommended for discharge, 3 were given complete exemption, 281 conditional exemption and 20 received noncombatant duty. Still another 1,202 cases arose on refusal of medical examination, in which the appellate tribunals found 457 not to be conscientious objectors and therefore liable to medical examination for the armed services, but granted complete exemption to 8, conditional exemption to 705, and noncombatant duty to 32.

The procedure at the appellate tribunal is entirely different from American procedure. In this country the claim is investigated secretly by the Federal Bureau of Investigation, heard *in camera* by a hearing officer without the registrant having any of the rights usually allowed in a court of law, and then on his recommendation decided by the appeal board solely on the papers filed by the registrant and the opinion of the hearing officer, and without the board ever seeing the registrant.

In Britain, appeal may be taken within 21 days after the decision of the local tribunal. Here we allowed only five days at first, now it is ten. The applicant in England is given the benefit of the written decision of the local tribunal and brief notes of the evidence, which are furnished him by the government. Here he may examine the file, but will find in it no record of the hearing, if any, and no reasons for the local board's decision.

As in America, the hearing in Britain is held whether or not the draftee puts in an appearance, but the British authorities send him a railway ticket from his home to the place of the hearing and pay all expenses involved for him and his witnesses to attend, whereas in America no expenses are paid and, distances being greater, many are prevented from attending and from bringing witnesses by the expense involved. It costs money to get justice in America.

The British appellate hearings are public; ours are private. The British consider the entire record of preceding events; our appeal boards consider only the recommendations of a hearing officer and the registrant's own documentary evidence. They do not have before them either the report of the investigation of the Federal Bureau of Investigation on which the hearing officer largely bases his decision, or the minutes of the testimony taken by the hearing officer, but must rely on his summation of the investigation and the testimony, thereby being restricted by his presentation and coloration of the facts. The appeal board in the United States never sees the registrant, nor the evidence, while in England the decision of the appellate tribunal is based on personal observation of the applicant and consideration of all the evidence.

In one further respect our procedure departs from orderly judicial forms which are so strictly followed in Britain: the decision of the appeal board may be reversed by the Director of Selective Service, to whom has been delegated this power by the President. This means that a single individual, the Director, is the final arbiter of conscientious objection. He is a General in the Army, and he acts with the dictatorial powers usual to his title. He holds no hearing, and gives no reasons for his decisions. Such a proceeding would be unthinkable in England, or for that matter in an America of a day less remote from the struggle for the rights won at Runnymede and Yorktown.

The treatment of conscientious objectors in prison does not vary greatly between England and the United States; although our prisons appear to be better in many respects. The typical British prison routine involves' some quaint customs, and some which hark back to medieval times. The prisoner is issued toilet articles when he enters prison, including a toothbrush bearing His Majesty's monogram, which he is told when he leaves the prison to preserve and bring with him if he should have to return. If he has been sentenced to "hard labour" the prisoner will be surprised to find that this does not mean work on the rock pile, but merely that he will sleep for a fortnight on a hard bed without a mattress, otherwise he is treated the same as other prisoners. Only the conservative mind of a Britisher, rooted in centuries of unchanging tradition, could continue to use the term hard labor to describe such punishment. Perhaps in the case of a woman prisoner in childbirth the term might be appropriate, but it is hardly relevant otherwise.

The daily routine of prison life is far more irksome than in America. We send most of our conscientious objectors to prisons for first offenders called "limited security" institutions, such as the prison at Danbury, Connecticut. They are allowed to work on the grounds outside the walls without even a guard, after establishing good conduct. A prisoner who wants to run away is free to depart, but few try it, as they are sure to be brought back and transferred to a less idyllic penitentiary. The theory is that four walls make a prison, even when the walls are intangible barriers to freedom, and that in the case of well-behaved prisoners no other restraint is necessary. But life in our prisons is nevertheless strictly disciplined, even at such prisons as Danubry, and in the older federal prisons many of the horrors of an earlier day persist.

At Springfield, Missouri, two conscientious objectors, as described in Chapter 8, were beaten by their guards, and although not mental cases, were placed alone and stark naked in "strip cells" designed for use with mental and emotional cases, where there was no furniture and only a hole in the floor for a toilet.

The British routine is far inferior to our limited security prisons, but not nearly so bad as the shameful strip cells of Springfield. The prisoner is unlocked in the morning to wash and shave, then locked up again while he takes breakfast in his cell. He then goes to the work-shop for the morning, returning to his cell for the mid-day meal, where he is locked up for an hour and a half. The afternoon is spent in the shop except for two half-hour exercise periods, when the prisoner is allowed to stretch his legs walking around a circular concrete track. After this, supper and the entire evening are spent locked in the cell. Under such a regimen, there is very little freedom to associate with other prisoners, and no recreation except what little can be had in the solitude of the cell. Except for the work in the shops, this is almost as bad as solitary confinement, and even at the work benches conversation is restricted.

Correspondence privileges are much more restricted than in the United States. Only one letter is allowed a month for the first period of imprisonment, later two a month can be sent. Furthermore, the prisoner can receive letters only in answer to the few he is allowed to write. By these standards American privileges of correspondence are munificent, although censorship exists here as abroad.

British prisoners may receive frequent visits from representatives of prisoners' aid societies, which continue even after release for the purpose of readjustment to civilian life. Weekly visits by a clergyman are also arranged for all who want this service.

The comparative number of prison sentences in Britain is much less than here, primarily because our law grants much narrower exemption, and also because our law has been narrowly applied by draft authorities and our procedure is more conducive to error.

About 2,000 conscientious objectors have been imprisoned in the United States out of about 12,000 claiming exemption, namely 16⅔ per cent, whereas about 60,000 Britishers have claimed to be conscientious objectors but only about 3,000 have been imprisoned, or about 5 per cent. In other words, more than three times as many conscientious objectors are imprisoned here as in England. But this does not take into account the fact that about two-thirds of the men imprisoned in the United States are in a class by themselves, the Jehovah's Witnesses, who demand complete exemption, which our law does not allow. H. N. Brailsford has remarked that the Jehovah's Witnesses would be in the forefront of a fight under the Lord God of Hosts at Armageddon, but will not fight in any other conflict or under any other general. The detailed figures* on British prosecutions up to June 1, 1943, are as follows:

Refusal of medical examination:
Imprisoned 1,813
Submitted to examination 208
           Total 2,021

Court martial for refusal to serve:
Once convicted 235
Twice convicted 112
Three times convicted 38
Four times convicted 2
Five times convicted 2
           Total 389

Other offenses:
Court martial after becoming a con-
conscientious objector while in the
service 88
Refusal to do "fire-watch" 297
Non-compliance with work condition 151
Refusal to register 16
Refusal to comply with industrial
conscription 169
Refusal to serve in home guard 18
Miscellaneous 28
           Total 767

Both the shortcomings of our treatment of conscien-

---

* Taken from published records of the Central Board for Conscientious Objectors, London.

tious objectors and the superiority on the whole of British handling of the same problem appears clearly from the foregoing comparison. The differences are due not to a British capacity for tolerance which exceeds our own, but to a greater familiarity with and understanding of the point of view of a minority. After all it is a rare individual indeed who can sympathize with and make allowances for a minority which he does not understand, and human nature being what it is, most of us will not go out of our way to gain the understanding necessary to a proper attitude toward those of different persuasion from ourselves.

In the British Isles the conscientious objector may not be any better liked than he is here but he is much more numerous, more vocal, and better understood. This has made it possible for the government to lay out a broad-minded program for conscientious objectors, and to administer it in fairness, with full popular support. Conversely, lack of knowledge led our government into the adoption of a program which is woefully inadequate, and lack of popular understanding is responsible for the Director of Selective Service having administered the program badly in order to maintain good relations with critical sections of the public.

Most of the credit for the excellent showing made by the British in these matters belongs in the first instance to the man who was so discredited for his handling of the war, Neville Chamberlain. He insisted on sensible treatment of conscientious objectors, on the theory that they were not wanted in the armed forces and should therefore be allowed to do work of value to the nation which their consciences would allow. Our law, on the other hand, was drafted without a single champion coming forward to support conscientious objection from either the administration or the Congress. It was only after a distinguished group of church and civic leaders descended on congressional committees that any exemption beyond the negligible one for pacifist religious sects was obtained. And even then, the Congressmen and the War Department had so little of statesmanship to offer in this regard that the inadequacies of the law they drafted have sent many hundreds to prison. The regulations were similarly drafted without reference to the lessons of history, or a decent regard to the well being of the men involved.

Compare this sorry record of a hasty improvisation gotten together by a disinterested Congress and Executive, with what happened in the British Parliament, where Lord Snell voiced the general opinion when he said:

"I hope that the time will never come when my nation will lack citizens who place their conception of right and duty above all other considerations—above derision, above penalties, and above discomforts. I cannot help feeling that it is a good thing and helpful to all of us that there should be in our midst a moral witness against the fundamental evil of war."*

---

* Central Board for Conscientious Objectors, London, Bulletin, April, 1911.

Conclusion

MANY OF THE problems discussed in this study reveal hostility on the part of the public toward conscientious objectors, and a lack of appreciation for the sincerity and high moral purpose by which they are motivated, and on the part of the conscientious objectors themselves a truculence and bitterness born of oppression. Although such sentiments as these are often characteristic of the struggle of a minority for recognition, they are neither important nor significant.

But there is a thread of light which is woven through this story, and it is both important and significant.

Although engaged in the most dangerous war of all history, our government, and the people who are its constituents, have granted legal recognition to conscientious objection. Not only does the law recognize that freedom of conscience is worthy of protection, but the attempt has been made to apply legal processes to the classification of conscientious objectors and to allow them to serve the nation in ways comparable to the service of the soldier. This is a great achievement for civil liberty in wartime, and when viewed as a part of the entire picture of civil liberty today, augurs well for the future. If we can preserve freedom and protect minorities in wartime, we are in no immediate danger of succumbing to the virus of totalitarianism.

While the principle of freedom of conscience has been written into the law, the principle has not always been applied. Out of the welter of bureaucracy which pervades the administration of the draft law, in common with other federal departments, have risen some of the injustices recounted in these pages. This is but another manifestation of the terrible disease which appears to have a firm grip on official Washington, and which has caused such sickness in domestic affairs. The body politic will never become well again until we return once more to the principle of government by laws and not by men. We are now being governed by men, the men who write the regulations that flow in vast streams from the fountainhead of government. No popular voice has any remote part in the framing of these regulations, and although they have the force of law, they are not in truth laws, but decrees. Most of the failures which have attended the treatment of conscientious objectors seem to come from this source. And they are no worse than many other failures in domestic affairs. With the passing of time and the sway of political fortunes, they will surely disappear.

It appears, then, that the successes of legal recognition for conscientious objection are an indication of a healthy society, while the failures are due to transitory troubles which afflict government in general. From these facts both the conscientious objector, and the public, may take heart.

Appendix I

Excerpt from
Selective Training and Service Act of 1940

SECTION 5 (g) Nothing contained in this Act shall be construed to require any person to be subject to combatant training and service in the land or naval forces of the United States who, by reason of religious training and belief, is conscientiously opposed to participation in war in any form. Any such person claiming such exemption from combatant training and service because of such conscientious objections whose claim is sustained by the local board shall, if he is inducted into the land or naval forces under this Act, be assigned to noncombatant service as defined by the President, or shall, if he is found to be conscientiously opposed to participation in such noncombatant service, in lieu of such induction, be assigned to work of national importance under civilian direction. Any such person claiming such exemption from combatant training and service because of such conscientious objections shall, if such claim is not sustained by the local board, be entitled to an appeal to the appropriate appeal board provided for in section 10 (a) (2). Upon the filing of such appeal with the appeal board, the appeal board shall forthwith refer the matter to the Department of Justice for inquiry and hearing by the Department or the proper agency thereof. After appropriate inquiry by such agency, a hearing shall be held by the Department of Justice with respect to the character and good faith of the objections of the person concerned, and such person shall be notified of the time and place of such hearing. The Department shall, after such hearing, if the objections are found to be sustained, recommend to the appeal board (1) that if the objector is inducted into the land or naval forces under this Act, he shall be assigned to noncombatant service as defined by the President, or (2) that if the objector is found to be conscientiously opposed to participation in such noncombatant service, he shall in lieu of such induction be assigned to work of national importance under civilian direction. If after such hearing the Department finds that his objections are not sustained, it shall recommend to the appeal board that such objections be not sustained. The appeal board shall give consideration to but shall not be bound to follow the recommendation of the Department of Justice together with the record on appeal from the local board in making its decision. Each person whose claim for exemption from combatant training and service because of conscientious objections is sustained shall be listed by the local board on a register of conscientious objectors.

Appendix II

Excerpts from
Selective Service Regulations

622.12 CLASS I-A-O: AVAILABLE FOR NONCOMBATANT MILITARY SERVICE; CONSCIENTIOUS OBJECTOR. In Class I-A-O shall be placed every registrant who would have been classified in Class I-A but for the fact that he has been found, by reason of religious training and belief, to be conscientiously opposed to participation in war in any form and to be conscientiously opposed to combatant military service in which he might be ordered to take human life, but not conscientiously opposed to noncombatant military service in which he could contribute to the health, comfort, and preservation of others.

622.51 CLASS IV-E: AVAILABLE FOR WORK OF NATIONAL IMPORTANCE; CONSCIENTIOUS OBJECTOR. (a) In Class IV-E shall be placed every registrant who would have been classified in Class I-A but for the fact that he has been found, by reason of religious training and belief, to be conscientiously opposed to participation in war in any form and to be conscientiously opposed to both combatant and noncombatant military service.

(b) Upon being advised by the Director of Selective Service that a registrant who was inducted into the land or naval forces for military service will be discharged because of conscientious objections which make him unadaptable to military service, the local board shall change such registrant's classification and place him in Class IV-E. The Director of Selective Service shall assign such registrant to work of national importance under civilian direction.

623.62   REGISTER OF CONSCIENTIOUS OBJECTORS. The local board shall list on a register of conscientious objectors each registrant whose claim for special classification as a conscientious objector has been sustained, either by the local board or upon appeal. The register of conscientious objectors shall show separately those registrants who have been classified as available for noncombatant military service (Class I-A-O) and those who have been classified as available for work of national importance under civilian direction only (Class IV-E). No special form is provided for this register.

627.25   SPECIAL PROVISIONS WHERE APPEAL INVOLVES CLAIM THAT REGISTRANT IS A CONSCIENTIOUS OBJECTOR. (a) If an appeal involves the question of whether or not a registrant is entitled to be sustained in his claim that he is a conscientious objector, the board of appeal shall first determine whether the registrant should be classified in one of the classes set forth in section 623.21, in the order set forth, and if it so determines, it shall place such registrant in such class. If the board of appeal does not determine that such registrant belongs in one of such classes, it shall transmit the entire file to the United States district attorney for the judicial district in which the local board of the registrant is located for the purpose of securing an advisory recommendation of the Department of Justice, provided that in a case in which the local board has classified the registrant in Class IV-E or in a case in which the registrant has claimed objection to combatant service only and the local board has classified him in Class I-A-O, the board of appeal may affirm the classification of the local board without referring the case to the Department of Justice. No registrant's file shall be forwarded to the United States district attorney by any board of appeal and any file so forwarded shall be returned, unless in the "Minutes of Other Actions" on the Selective Service Questionnaire (Form 40) the record shows and the letter of transmittal states that the board of appeal reviewed the file and determined that the registrant should not be classified in one of the classes set forth in section 623.21.

(b) The Department of Justice shall thereupon make an inquiry and hold a hearing on the character and good faith of the conscientious objections of the registrant. The registrant shall be notified of the time and place of such hearing and shall have an opportunity to be heard. If the objections of the registrant are found to be sustained, the Department of Justice shall recommend to the board of appeal (1) that if the registrant is inducted into the land or naval forces, he shall be assigned to noncombatant service, or (2) that if the registrant is found to be conscientiously opposed to participation in such noncombatant service, he shall be assigned to work of national importance under civilian direction. If the Department of Justice finds that the objections of the registrant are not sustained, it shall recommend to the board of appeal that such objections be not sustained.

(c) Upon receipt of the report of the Department of Justice, the board of appeal shall determine the classification of the registrant, and in its determination it shall give consideration to, but it shall not be bound to follow, the recommendation of the Department of Justice.

643.1 PAROLE: GENERAL. Any person who has heretofore or may hereafter be convicted of a violation of any of the provisions of the Selective Training and Service Act of 1940, or any amendment thereto, or any rules or regulations prescribed thereunder, shall at any time after such conviction be eligible for parole for service in the land or naval forces of the United States, or for work of national importance under civilian direction, or for any other special service established pursuant to said act, in the manner and under the conditions hereinafter set out.

643.2 PAROLE OF PERSON REQUIRED TO REGISTER. The parole provided for in section 643.1 may be granted by the Attorney General to any person required to register under the provisions of the Selective Training and Service Act of 1940, as amended, and any proclamation of the President thereunder, if in the judgment of the Attorney General it is compatible with the public interest and the enforcement of the Selective Training and Service Act of 1940, as amended, upon the recommendation of the Director of Selective Service. Before recommending the parole of any such person, the Director of Selective Service shall determine and include in his recommendation whether such person should be paroled for (1) induction into the land or naval forces of the United States; or (2) induction into the land or naval forces of the United States for noncombatant service, as such service has been or may hereafter be defined; or (3) assignment to work of national importance under civilian direction in lieu of induction into the land or naval forces of the United States; or (4) assignment to such other special service as may be established by the Attorney General pursuant to the Selective Training and Service Act of 1940, as amended. If the parole is granted, it shall conform to such recommendation.

651.1 SELECTION OF REGISTRANTS FOR ASSIGNMENT TO WORK OF NATIONAL IMPORTANCE. Every registrant who is classified in Class IV-E, before he is assigned to work of national importance under civilian direction, shall be given a final-type physical examination for registrants in Class IV-E. Each such registrant shall be ordered to report for such examination when his order number is reached in the process of selecting Class I-A and Class I-A-O registrants to report for induction, provided his classification is not under consideration on appearance, reopening, or appeal, and the time in which he is entitled to request an appearance or take an appeal has expired.

652.14 PERIOD OF SERVICE. (a) A registrant in Class IV-E who has been assigned to a camp shall be engaged in work of national importance under civilian direction during the existence of any war in which the United States is engaged and during the 6 months immediately following the termination of any such war, unless sooner released under the same conditions as pertain in the armed forces.

(b) A person assigned to a camp on parole pursuant to part 643 shall be engaged in work of national importance under civilian direction for the length of the term of his sentence less deductions for good conduct as provided in part 643.

653.1 WORK PROJECTS. (a) The Director of Selective Service is authorized to establish, designate, or determine work of national importance under civilian direction. He may establish, designate, or determine, by an appropriate order, projects which he deems to be work of national importance. Such projects will be identified by number and may be referred to as "civilian public service camps."

(b) Each work project will be under the civilian direction of the United States Department of Agriculture, United States Department of the Interior, or such other Federal, State, or local governmental or private agency as may be designated by the Director of Selective Service. Each such agency will hereinafter be referred to as the "technical agency."

(c) The responsibility and authority for supervision and control over all work projects is vested in the Director of Selective Service.

653.2 CAMPS. (a) The Director of Selective Service may arrange for the establishment of a camp at any project designated as work of national importance under civilian direction.

(b) Government-operated camps may be established in which the work of national importance and camp operations will both be under the civilian direction of a Federal technical agency using funds provided by the Selective Service System and operating under such camp rules as may be prescribed by the Director of Selective Service.

(c) The Director of Selective Service may authorize the National Service Board for Religious Objectors, a voluntary unincorporated association of religious organizations, to operate camps. The work project for assignees of such camps will be under the civilian direction of a technical agency. Such camps and work projects shall be operated under such camp rules as may be prescribed by the Director of Selective Service.

653.3   PROPERTY AND FINANCE. (a) The Director of Selective Service will allot funds to each technical agency having supervision over a work project. Such funds may be obligated and expended by such technical agencies in accordance with the laws, rules, and regulations governing expenditures by the Selective Service System, except in cases where the Director of Selective Service specifically authorizes the technical agency to obligate and expend such funds for a particular purpose in accordance with the laws, rules, and regulations governing the usual activities of such technical agency. Not later than the 10th day of each month the representative, designated for such purpose by each technical agency receiving funds allotted by the Director of Selective Service, shall prepare a Report of Obligations (Form 260 and supplements) showing all funds obligated by such agency during the preceding month and shall distribute the original and copies of such forms in accordance with instructions thereon.

(b) The technical agency receiving property or equipment purchased from funds allotted by the Director of Selective Service shall designate a representative who shall be the responsible and the accountable officer.

(c) The National Service Board for Religious Objectors shall designate a representative as the responsible and accountable officer for and shall post a sufficient bond to indemnify the United States against loss of or damage to all camp buildings, camp-operating equipment, and other Government-owned property loaned to the non-Federal group in connection with the operation of any of its camps.

(d) When the National Service Board for Religious Objectors has been authorized to operate a camp, it shall assume the entire financial responsibility for the wages of the camp director and other employees, the clothing, feeding, housing, medical care, hospitalization, welfare, and recreation of assignees and all other costs of operating the camp.

(e) The Director of Selective Service is authorized to pay assignees in Government-operated camps. The pay of assignees shall not be more than $5 per month except that not to exceed 6 percent of the assignees may be paid not more than $7.50 per month. The Director of Selective Service is also authorized to provide subsistence, proper clothing for the performance of their duties, and such other personal supplies or equipment as he deems necessary for assignees in Government-operated camps, without expense to such assignees.

(f) The purchase and procurement of food, supplies, clothing, and equipment; the maintenance and repair of buildings and equipment; the pay of administrative personnel; the pay of assignees; the incurring of other obligations; and other expenditures in connection with Government-operated camps will be made (1) in accordance with the laws, rules, and regulations governing such transactions within the Selective Service System or (2) when specifically authorized for a particular purpose by the Director of Selective Service, in accordance with the laws, rules, and regulations governing the usual activities of such technical agency.

653.12 DUTIES. Assignees shall report to the camp to which they are assigned; remain therein until released or transferred elsewhere by proper authority, except when performing assigned duties or on authorized missions or leave outside of camp; perform their assigned duties promptly and efficiently; keep their persons, clothing, equipment, and quarters neat and clean; conserve and protect Government property; conduct themselves both in and outside of the camp so as to bring no discredit to the individual or the organization; and comply with such camp rules as may be prescribed or such directions as may be issued from time to time by the Director of Selective Service.

Appendix III

Excerpts from the British "National Service (Armed Forces) Act" of 1939 Effective September 3, 1939

5. (1) If any person liable under this act to be called up for service claims that he conscientiously objects—

(a) To being registered in the military service register, or

(b) To performing military service, or

(c) To performing combatant duties,

he may, on furnishing the prescribed particulars about himself, apply in the prescribed manner to be registered as a conscientious objector in a special register to be kept by the Minister (hereinafter referred to as "the register of conscientious objectors"); provided, that where, in the case of a person who has been medically examined under this act, such an application as aforesaid is made more than 2 days after the completion of his medical examination, the Minister shall dismiss the application unless he is satisfied, having regard to the grounds on which the application is made, that the making thereof has not been unreasonably delayed.

(2) Where any person duly makes application to be registered in the register of conscientious objectors, he shall, unless his application is dismissed in accordance with the proviso to the last foregoing subsection, be provisionally registered in that register.

(3) A person who has been provisionally registered in the register of conscientious objectors shall, within the prescribed period and in the prescribed manner, make to a local tribunal constituted under part I of the schedule to this act an application stating to which of the matters mentioned in paragraphs (a) to (c) of subsection (1) of this section he conscientiously objects, and, if he fails to do so, the Minister

shall remove his name from the register of conscientious objectors.

(4) An applicant for registration as a conscientious objector who is aggrieved by any order of a local tribunal, and the Minister, if he considers it necessary, may, within the prescribed time and in the prescribed manner, appeal to the appellate tribunal constituted under part I of the schedule of this act, and the decision of the appellate tribunal shall be final.

(5) The Minister or any person authorized by him shall be entitled to be heard on any application or appeal to a tribunal under this section.

(6) A local tribunal, if satisfied, upon an application duly made to it under this section, or the appellate tribunal, if satisfied on appeal, that the ground upon which the application was made is established, shall by order direct either—

(a) That the applicant shall, without conditions, be registered in the register of conscientious objectors; or

(b) That he shall be conditionally registered in that register until the end of the present emergency, the condition being that he must until that event undertake work specified by the tribunal, of a civil character and under civilian control and, if directed by the Minister, undergo training provided or approved by the Minister to fit him for such work; or

(c) That his name shall be removed from the register of conscientious objectors and that he shall be registered as a person liable under this act to be called up for service but to be employed only in noncombatant duties; but, if not so satisfied, shall by order direct that his name shall, without qualification, be removed from the register of conscientious objectors.

(7) The minister may provisionally register in the register of conscientious objectors any person liable under this act to be called up for service, notwithstanding that he has refused or failed to make any application in that behalf, if in the

Minister's opinion there are reasonable grounds for thinking that he is a conscientious objector, and the Minister may refer the case of that person to a local tribunal, and thereupon the provisions of this section shall have effect in relation to that person as if the necessary applications had been made by him, and references in this section to the "applicant" shall be deemed to include references to him.

(8) If on the information of any person, a local tribunal is satisfied that any person who is conditionally registered in the register of conscientious objectors by virtue of a direction given under paragraph (b) of subsection (6) of this section has failed to observe that condition, the local tribunal shall report the fact to the Minister, who shall require him to make a fresh application to a local tribunal, and upon any such application that tribunal may deal with him in like manner as, after being satisfied that the ground of his application was established, they had power to deal with him on his original application, but if he fails to make such a fresh application when required by the Minister, the Minister shall forthwith remove his name from the register of conscientious objectors and register him as a person liable under this act to be called up for service but to be employed only in noncombatant duties.

(9) If, while a person is conditionally registered in the register of conscientious objectors, any change occurs in the particulars about him entered in that register, he shall forthwith notify the change to the Minister in the prescribed manner, and if he fails to do so shall be liable on summary conviction to a fine not exceeding £5; and the Minister may remove his name from the register of conscientious objectors and register him as a person liable under this act to be called up for service but to be employed only in noncombatant duties.

(10) A person shall not be liable under this act to be called up for service so long as he is registered in the register of conscientious objectors; and the admiralty, army council,

and air council, shall make arrangements for securing that, where a person registered as a person liable under this act to be called up for service, but to be employed only in noncombatant duties is called up under this act for service, he shall, during the period for which he serves by virtue of being so called up, be employed only in such duties.

(11) The regulations made under this act regulating the procedure of such tribunals as aforesaid shall make provision for the appellate tribunal to sit in two divisions, of which one shall sit for Scotland, and shall empower the tribunals to take evidence on oath, and shall make provision as to the representation of parties to proceedings before the tribunals which shall include the right to appear either in person or by counsel or a solicitor or by a representative of any trade union to which they belong or by any person who satisfies such a tribunal that he is a relative or personal friend of the party he proposes to represent.

(12) No determination of a local tribunal or the appellate tribunal made for the purposes of this act shall be called in question in any court of law.

(13) The Minister may pay—

(a) To members of tribunals constituted under this section such remuneration and allowances as he may, with the approval of the treasury, determine; and

(b) To applicants appearing before such tribunals, and to any witnesses whose attendance is certified by any such tribunal to have been necessary, traveling and subsistence allowances in accordance with such scale as the Minister may, with the consent of the treasury, approve; and

(c) To persons undergoing training in accordance with directions given by the Minister under paragraph (b) of subsection (6) of this section training allowances in accordance with such scale as he may, with the consent of the treasury, approve.

Index